You and Your Marriage

by

HUGH B. BROWN

Bookcraft
Salt Lake City, Utah

Foreword

Elder Hugh B. Brown, one of the stalwarts of the Church, and one, who through love and study, knows what goes on in the minds and hearts of young and old, has prepared *You and Your Marriage* for the thoughtful consideration of youth themselves.

From a life rich in experience as an exponent of youth, Elder Brown builds a heartwarming marriage handbook into a fabric of truth that will lead youth to accept the inevitability of the principles he advocates. Because of Elder Brown's rare and fascinating approach, youth feels confidence in his conclusions.

You and Your Marriage goes to its readers with the considered and tempered judgment and love of one who, having with his wife, reared eight children of his own, extends his fatherly concern to all youth everywhere. If young people will put into practice these thoughtful and pertinent directives, marriage will become an enduring partnership of beauty and happiness.

March 9, 1960

Marba C. Josephson

Contents

Preface

The writer of these notes is not a psychiatrist, a psychologist, nor a medical practitioner. He writes only as one who has had some experience through the years, both secular and ecclesiastical, with both pre-marital and post-marital counseling. Alarming statistics and daily experience with those who have marital problems makes one wish he could add a helpful word of caution, instruction, and encouragement.

While he is acutely aware of the fact that he can scarcely hope to add any new thoughts to this age-old subject, perhaps repetition may emphasize and focus attention. These simple essays are written from the practical point of view of a father and grandfather, a friend and counselor of youth. The excuse for writing is the conviction that a large percentage of marriage failures could have been avoided if, figuratively, the drivers—both front and back seat drivers—had taken some elementary instruction and passed some simple tests before being allowed to "take the wheel." In auto or air travel, it is imperative that only one at a time have hold of the wheel or the controls. To wrestle for control while the vehicle is in motion is dangerous to the would-be drivers and may prove fatal to innocent passengers.

The first questions a rescue team ask when they find the ruins of a car or plane after a crash are, "What went wrong?" "Who was responsible?" and the heartbreaking answer generally is, "It could have been avoided." We who investigate and try to repair matrimonial wreckage usually reach the same conclusion: It might have been avoided.

Having officiated at many marriage ceremonies, both civil and ecclesiastical, and having, by appointment, investigated and tried to save and succor thousands of "shipwrecked mariners" who, feeling discouraged, disillusioned, and defeated, have from time to time sent out an urgent SOS, the writer wishes to share with others some of the lessons learned along the way.

Also the prayerful hope is expressed that some who are about to "set sail" may chance to read and possibly heed a word of warning and direction from one who has learned some lessons on the sea of matrimony for more than fifty years.

The "Mate" in this case has valiantly stood at the helm beside the "Captain" through high seas and stormy weather, without flinching or complaining. She now nestles with him in the harbor and sweetly whispers, "It was worth it. I'd do it all again." To her, a most successful matrimonial mariner, this little book is gratefully dedicated.

I. Marriage Instituted by God, Therefore Eternal

The LDS Concept of Marriage

Marriage is and should be a sacrament. The word *sacrament* is variously defined, but among Christian people it signifies a religious act or ceremony, solemnized by one having proper authority. It is a pledge, or solemn covenant, a spiritual sign or bond between the contracting parties themselves and between them and God. That marriage was instituted and sanctified by the Lord Himself is shown by the following quotations:

> And the Lord God said, it is not good that the man should be alone; I will make him an help meet for him.

> Therefore shall a man leave his father and his mother, and shall cleave unto his wife: and they shall be one flesh. —Genesis 2:18, 24

When Jesus departed from Galilee and came into the coasts of Judea beyond Jordan, a great multitude followed him, and the Pharisees questioned him regarding divorce.

> And he answered and said unto them, Have ye not read, that he which made them at the beginning made them male and female.

> And said, For this cause shall a man leave father and mother, and shall cleave to his wife: and they twain shall be one flesh.

> Wherefore they are no more twain, but one flesh. What therefore God hath joined together, let not man put asunder. —Matthew 19:4-6

It is plain that God intended that man and woman should become one. By personally officiating at this first wedding He sanctified the institution of marriage. It is a normal, healthful, and desirable state and was instituted to fulfil God's purpose in the earth.

It is the central element in the domestic establishment. It is more than a human institution to be regulated solely by custom and civil law. It is more than a contract under the sanction of moral law. It is or should be a religious sacrament by which men and women solemnly undertake to co-operate with God in His avowed purpose to make earth life and mortality available to His spirit children and to bring to pass their immortality and eternal life.

There are those who say that the highest, most dedicated, and most desirable life may be achieved outside the marriage covenant. In other words they would forbid those who seek the highest glory to be "contaminated by physical and animal-like associations." There is no warrant in the scripture for such doctrine. In the book of Proverbs we read:

> Whoso findeth a wife findeth a good thing, and obtaineth favour of the Lord.
>
> —Proverbs 18:22

and the apostle in writing to Timothy, said:

> Now the Spirit speaketh expressly, that in the latter times some shall depart from the faith, giving heed to seducing spirits, and doctrines of devils; Speaking lies in hypocrisy; having their conscience seared with a hot iron;
>
> Forbidding to marry, and commanding to abstain from meats, which God hath created to be re-

ceived with thanksgiving of them which believe
and know the truth.

—I Timothy 4:1-3

and in the Doctrine and Covenants we read:

And again, verily I say unto you that whoso for-
biddeth to marry is not ordained of God, for marriage is ordained of God unto man.

—D&C 49:15

The Latter-day Saints believe that in order to attain the
best in life and the greatest happiness in this world and the
next, men and women must be married in the temple for
time and eternity. Without the sealing ordinances of temple
marriage, man cannot achieve a Godlike stature or receive a
fulness of joy because the unmarried person is not a whole
person, is not complete.

To a Latter-day Saint there is only one kind of marriage which is wholly acceptable, that is, temple or celestial
marriage, which is performed only in the temples of the
Church. Temples are erected and dedicated in holiness to
the Lord to provide a place where spiritual and eternal
ceremonies and ordinances may be performed. While we
recognize civil marriages performed by ministers of other
churches, and civil marriages performed by officers of the
law, or others legally qualified to perform them, we believe
that only in a temple of God can a marriage for time and
eternity be performed, and then only by one having the
authority which Christ gave to Peter when he said:

. . . whatsoever thou shalt bind on earth shall be
bound in heaven: . . .

—Matthew 16:19

This authority is referred to in the scriptures as "the keys of the kingdom of heaven," (Matthew 16:19) and in celestial marriage those keys open the door to that kingdom.

Man has certain basic needs, moral, social, biological, and spiritual, and these can only be fully realized in the God-ordained institution of eternal marriage.

To live the abundant life here and eternal life hereafter, man must love and be loved, serve and sacrifice, have responsibility and exercise his God-given creative powers. "I am come that they might have life, and that they might have it more abundantly."

But perhaps the greatest value of marriage is not that which accrues to the individual man and woman. The purpose of their union in the beginning is indicated by the Lord's commandment, "Be fruitful, and multiply, and replenish the earth, and subdue it: . . ." (Genesis 1:28) In proper marriage there is opportunity for man to realize his natural urge to be creative and productive. This can be completely fulfilled and properly enjoyed only in the marriage relationship, in child bearing and child rearing. Parents should remember that the children born to them— their children—are also the children of God. He is the Father of their spirit bodies, and during the pre-earth existence He wisely made provision for eternal element and eternal spirit to be inseparably connected and receive a fulness of joy. Latter-day Saints therefore believe that God is actually the third partner in this relationship, and that bringing children into the world within the divinely sanctioned institution of marriage is part of His plan to bring to pass the immortality and eternal life of man.

When the Lord Jesus designated love of God and love of fellow men as the two great commandments, he glorified love. In fact, we are told that God is love. Therefore as God is eternal, so love must be eternal, and its fruits and blessings are intended to continue throughout the eternities to come. But to enjoy the privileges and advantages of eternal love as it relates to husbands and wives, parents and children, the ordinance which authorizes and sanctifies this most beautiful of all relationships is not acceptable if it contains the limitation "until death do you part." For family relationship and conjugal associations to be eternal, the marriage contract must *authoritatively* state, "for time and for all eternity."

All people should realize their responsibility to their offspring and to the covenants they make with respect thereto. When the Lord said, "We without them cannot be made perfect." (D&C 128:18.) He was referring to a chain whose links extend into the future as well as the past. In fact, we may have more direct responsibility for those entrusted to us in this life than to our ancestors. We cannot be held responsible for the sins, either of commission or of omission of our ancestors, but He has warned that in case of failure on the part of our posterity, if it can be attributed to our failure in our duty to them, then the sins will be upon our heads.

Among the blessings of those who attain the highest degree in the celestial kingdom is the blessing of eternal increase, which, among other things, means that even after death men may continue to co-operate with God in bringing to pass the immortality and eternal life of man.

The Latter-day Saint concept of eternal progression includes eternal development, eternal increase of knowledge, power, intelligence, awareness, and all the characteristics and capacities which make for Godhood. But in the economy of God men cannot attain this state of continuing perfection in his unfinished or unmarried state. There must be growth and increase of the whole man, in other words, the man, who has found and been united to his other half.

This concept of marriage, with its divine perspective, gives new meaning and adds importance, dignity, and glory to the idea of marriage. With this concept the thoughtful person will be more careful and selective in the choice of his eternal companion. Certainly before entering into such an eternal contract both men and women should be humble and thoughtful, and should prayerfully seek for divine guidance.

The religious sanctity and sanction of the marriage relationship is greatly enhanced and appreciated where the couple, before marriage—and they must, necessarily, be of the same faith—start with the same goal in mind. They must prepare and be worthy to receive the sacred ordinance in edifices where only the worthy may enter. Here they receive instruction, make covenants, and then at the altar pledge eternal love and fidelity, each for the other, in the presence of God and of angels. Surely such a concept and practice, with its accompanying obligations, makes for the permanence of the home, the glorifying of the institution of marriage, and the salvation of the souls of men.

Such marriage is essentially an act of faith, solemnized in the presence of a divine partner. There must be faith and courage to see it through, to endure to the end, despite

the difficulties, trials, disappointments, and occasional be-reavements which may be encountered.

When one accepts the conditions and obligations of this eternal partnership, he must realize that failure here is almost total failure. Whatever his successes may be in other fields of activity, if a man fails to discharge the obligations imposed by this eternal covenant, the appalling penalty will be the loss of celestial glory, accompanied by responsibility for the losses sustained by those with whom he made the contract and for whom he is responsible.

. . . marriage is ordained of God unto man.

Wherefore, it is lawful that he should have one wife, and they twain shall be one flesh, and all this that the earth might answer the end of its creation; And that it might be filled with the measure of man, according to his creation before the world was made.

—D&C 49:15-17

Why Marriage

"Thy wife shall be as a fruitful vine by the side of thine house: thy children like olive plants round about thy table."

—Psalm 128:3

Sometimes, at the close of the day, the weary marriage counselor feels almost to echo the question so often asked during interviews with people who are not truly married but simply undivorced; a question which has been repeated in all generations through the ages, namely, "Why marriage?"

Some have asked, why, in the face of the fact that there is so much suffering in and through marriage, we should continue to encourage it. Here, as in all cases where questions arise concerning the laws and institutions in our civilization, when someone suggests that we do away with or change certain established policies, customs, or institutions, the logical question is, "What is the alternative?"

Marriage, to all believers in the Holy Scriptures, is a sacred institution, established by the Lord Himself, to promote the happiness and well-being of His children. To the truly religious person, the fact that God Himself commanded His children to multiply and replenish the earth is sufficient answer to the question: "Why?" In other words, we marry because it is a commandment of God, a part of His divine plan, and all of His commandments are for the good and benefit of mankind. Here, as elsewhere in the great plan of

salvation the ultimate blessings come only to those who
endure to the end. The promised blessings are not bestowed
at the marriage altar, but must be earned through patient
years.

Let us for a moment consider our second question,
"What would be an alternative to marriage?" Think of a
world or a society without marriage. Think of the plight
of little children, if there were no marriage vows to bind
their parents together, no homes in which they could know
the security of filial affection. There, of course, would be
children, even if there were no marriage, for mortal men
and women are endowed with creative and procreative instincts and with a natural love of love, and with a God-given
impulse to give in love. The absence of marriage would play
havoc with the social order and undermine the very foundation of our civilization.

We must admit at the outset that there are many
unhappy marriages, but if they who contemplate this most
glorifying and intimate of all human relationships would
seek to qualify for its responsibilities; would refuse to rush
headlong into it without preparation; and then refuse to
rush to the emergency exit, divorce, when trouble or discord
appear; if they would take time to get acquainted with their
proposed partner and prayerfully seek divine guidance; if
the partners would discuss together before marriage the
serious problems involved therein, anticipating together and
agreeing on procedures, ambitions, and goals, would inquire
into each other's background, their ancestry, nationality,
church affiliation and activity; if they would frankly discuss
the delicate and sanctifying aspects of harmonious sex life
which are involved in marriage; if, in other words, people

would prepare for marriage as they prepare for the practice of law, medicine, or any vocation of life, much sorrow, heartbreak, and tragedy could be avoided.

There is such a thing as ideal marriage, but it cannot be fully realized in the brief honeymoon which follows the wedding although the seeds of future happiness may be sown during that period. Marriage can and should lead to immor-tality and eternal life, the greatest of all God's gifts, to be fully enjoyed only when the family unit endures into eternity.

Celestial marriage is an everlasting covenant, prerequi-site to exaltation and eternal progress in the Kingdom of God. As God is love and as God is eternal, so love is eternal. True love never dies. Of all the ordinances of the Gospel of Jesus Christ, none is more sacred, more glorifying than celestial marriage.

The Lord said, "Man is not without the woman, neither the woman without the man in the Lord." There-fore, there can be no exaltation with the fulness of the blessings of celestial kingdom outside of the marriage relation. No man can be exalted singly and alone, neither can any woman.

We do not overlook or minimize the problems inherent in married life, especially those of us who have spent years in counseling, seeking to heal and to help. All marriage counselors, as well as most parents and church leaders are in varying degrees aware of what goes on "behind the scenes," but much of the marital unhappiness could be or could have been avoided if the parties thereto had been willing to play the game according to the rules, to make the same kind of allowance for the weaknesses in others

which they so readily make for themselves. Marriage requires many concessions, makes many demands, but in the
school of life there is no stronger educative factor.

Unfortunately women generally suffer more acutely
than men during and after the breakup of marriages. Man's
work gives him many outside interests; his nature makes
him more independent; and partly as a result of this, despite
his vows and obligations, he frequently seeks the path of
least resistance and cowardly abandons his companion, often
with little ones at her side, and thereby breaks one of the
first commandments. As love of neighbor is next to love
of God, surely love of family is a divine obligation.

If the man will let his wife know that she is loved and
appreciated, she will not only be happy and make whatever
sacrifices may be required of her, but she will help him
materially and mentally, shield him with her love and believe
in him when others doubt, will reinforce the link which
binds them together, and will be an efficient and loving
companion.

A strong mutual interest in some subject that appeals
to both with approximately equal force may become a very
effective means of offsetting, or at least bringing into proper
perspective, the little, though vexatious problems which
arise daily in married life. To have mutual hobbies and
outside interests, games or sports, or cultivating a garden,
will increase mutual sympathy and mutual regard.

But there is no mutual interest as efficacious and rewarding for the married couple as the rearing of a family,
caring for the children which they themselves have pro-
duced. This is an ancient truth which must not be disregarded. They who postpone or refuse to have children,

who shirk the added tasks that they might indulge selfish pleasures and comforts, are inviting shipwreck of their homes.

To the question, "Why Marriage?" we submit:

a. Because the Lord commands it.
b. Only through it can the purpose of life—joy—be fully realized.
c. It is the Lord's plan for the perpetuation of the race.
d. It is one of life's most rewarding and exalting disciplines.
e. It is absolutely necessary in the best interests of children.
f. Through it we learn the beauty of unselfish love and learn to lose ourselves in service.
g. Only through this gate may men and women enter the highest degree of glory in the celestial kingdom.

If much is suffered in and through marriage, without it humanity would suffer much more.

When Marriage

We are often asked the question, "What is a proper age for young people to marry?" There is, of course, no age at which each young person should marry, and we cannot therefore give a blanket answer to the question.

Calendar age or physical and biological development are not the only, or, in fact, the primary considerations. Marriage calls for physical, mental, moral, and spiritual adulthood or maturity. While it is not possible to say when a person is sufficiently mature to marry, there are many case histories of marriage failures due to immaturity. In the Western States, including Utah, there were almost one-third as many divorces as marriages in 1958. Three and one-half times as many teen-age marriages ended in divorce as in the 22-28 year group. Statistics show that 26 percent of all brides today are under eighteen and 47 percent under 19. Too often these young couples enter marriage as a game and do not realize they should be playing for keeps. With these statistics in mind, we ask, "What's the hurry?"

Marriage presupposes at least some measure of adulthood and maturity. Teen-agers are still in the process of maturing, physically, mentally, socially, psychologically, and spiritually. They are still in the transition stage, still growing and whatever their calendar age or physical size, they are still infants. When two such persons marry, if they continue to grow, they sometimes grow apart rather than together. If their interests, their objectives, and personalities

grow farther and farther apart, a break becomes inevitable. They who marry while still in the transition stage are gambling—with their own and others' happiness at stake.

They who are emotionally immature, childish, and cannot behave as grown-ups, should not assume life's most serious responsibility. Marriage is an enterprise for adults. They who do marry in infancy—and some infants are more than twenty years old—find themselves in almost constant conflict. In such cases each should go to work on himself rather than on his mate and try to fit himself into the pattern of a joint life. Much can be done by recognizing the problem, finding the source of the trouble and in a mature manner, undertaking to overcome and correct the habits, attitudes, and eccentricities with which he entered the new partnership.

Too many make the mistake of thinking mere infatua-tion is real love. Too many rush into marriage with the first one for whom they feel an emotional, and often fleeting, attraction. Short acquaintance, lack of dating experience, and failure to use the head as well as the heart are respon-sible for the fact that approximately one-half of all marriages of girls under nineteen years of age end in unhappiness, separation, or divorce.

"Love at first sight" should take a second and longer look in a less glamorous setting. The person who is the object of one's love should be examined against his or her background in search of a better understanding of his character. It is generally desirable that both parties to the intended contract should first have a relatively large number of so-called dates to enable them to choose rightly and wisely from among the larger group. In this way they will

learn to distinguish between passing infatuation and real affection. Real and lasting love is a developing relationship rather than an abrupt awakening and should be tested by acquaintance, friendship, and association.

The wise gourmet, when going into a first-class restaurant, asks for a complete list of what is available, takes time to study it, and then orders what experience has taught him will give pleasure, satisfaction, and sustenance without any sour after-effects. How much more discriminating he would be if he were selecting a daily diet for the balance of his life.

While physical attraction is essential to love between man and woman, it should not be allowed to become paramount. Mutual emotional responses do not guarantee love or assure a good marriage. Infatuation may be romantic, glamorous, thrilling, and even urgent, but genuine love should not be in a hurry. The young and immature are too often motivated by impulse and emotion. The young girl who ecstatically exclaims, "He has that certain something," may see the day when she will wish he had "something certain."

An eminent specialist and teacher recently said, "In many cases of teen-age marriage the couple is not looking for sexual thrills but for a secure niche in society. They want a nice, steady job, a regular income, a little home with gadgets. Sometimes they dash into marriage just to get away from parental authority."

Love is too precious, too rare, to be squandered merely as an expression of sexual pleasure or a need for security or means of rebellion. Real love can be the most positive force in life, but it requires maturity to know when it exists.

How often the hopes and wishful thinking of unwise and immature young people are wrecked in the quiet calm of better acquaintance, leaving heartache, emotional and spiritual scars, and sometimes ineradicable stains.

After marriage, mature judgment and wise decision are called for almost daily, and weighty problems must be met and solved. We speak not only of calendar age, or merely physical age, but also of actual maturity, mental, emotional, and spiritual. Statistics on marriage show that the best levels of adjustment are found when men marry between the ages of twenty-five and thirty and women between the ages of twenty-three and twenty-eight.

The Apostle Paul gave the best definition of love when he wrote, speaking of charity, or love:

> [Love] suffereth long, and is kind; . . . envieth not; . . . vaunteth not itself, is not puffed up.
>
> Doth not behave itself unseemly, . . . is not easily provoked, thinketh no evil;
>
> Rejoiceth not in iniquity, but rejoiceth in the truth;
>
> Beareth all things, believeth all things, hopeth all things, endureth all things.
>
> [Love] never faileth: . . .
>
> I Corinthians 13:4-8
>
> When I was a child, I spake as a child, I understood as a child, I thought as a child; but when I became a man, I put away childish things.
>
> —Ibid., 13:11

Frequently when parents or marriage counselors undertake to dissuade impetuous youth from sudden emotional decisions regarding marriage, they are met with the state-

ment, "But we are truly in love. We've been going steady, and we can't stand to be separated." We wonder how often they are blinded by the glittering diamond on the finger of a friend, or prodded by the boasting of the giver. But when circumstances, or call to duty, result in separa' tion—i.e. military or mission service — one or both of the parties frequently form new attachments, write "Dear John" letters, and are grateful that circumstances intervened and prevented what might have been a sad mistake.

And later when the same marriage counselors, again dealing with impetuous youth, are trying to dissuade them from sudden and emotional decisions regarding divorce, they hear the plaintive cry, "We're congenial in a way, but somehow our marriage isn't what we expected. We still love each other—we think—but things just don't go right. We had a beautiful wedding, and a wonderful honeymoon, but we aren't happy. Perhaps we should not have married at all."

Such people seemingly expected passionate and impet' uous association to continue unabated, without being fed, nurtured, and kept growing during storms as well as in sunshine. All living things need sustenance, and if they stop growing, they begin to die. Love is a very tender plant; when properly nourished, it becomes sturdy and enduring, but neglected it will soon wither and may die.

Childish love, though it be a sweet and beautiful thing at times, is often selfish and self'centered. Mature love, if it be real, desires not merely self'satisfaction, but thinks first of the satisfaction of the mate.

Many young couples overemphasize the seriousness of problems which arise in the first years of their marriage, and, in a sense, make "mountains out of molehills." This is not

to say there are not many very serious problems to meet and solve. But if they will consider such problems together, as adult people should, if they will bring all their misunder-standings out into the open, discuss them frankly, and in a sort of mutual compromise face up to the trouble zones in married life, pinpoint and analyze them, and keep them in proper perspective, they may discover that they have been looking through magnifying glasses.

Where there is deep and mature love, which is being nurtured and jealously guarded, the couple will confide in each other and discuss all matters of joint interest—and in marriage everything should be of interest to both—they will stand together in adversity, will lean on, support, and give strength to each other. They will find that their combined strength is more than double the strength of either one of them alone. Trouble and adversity, when jointly met, will strengthen the marriage and bind the couple together some-times more closely than if all the days were sunshine and ease. Just "talking things over" goes far toward reaching a solution, it keeps the couple in rapport but if the line of communication between husband and wife is severed, by sulking, or temper tantrums, what was once exuberance and joy give way to indifference, misunderstanding, and, if not corrected, active dislike and hatred. Inhibitions and weakened relationships can be avoided and stress and strain can make us stronger if met and handled on an adult level.

Sincerity and frankness are to marriage what honesty and integrity are to business. Their presence insures suc-cess; their absence leads to bankruptcy.

In view of all of this, again we should ask the question "What's the hurry?"

Whom to Marry

"In their spring of life, when fancy waved her fairy wand around them, till all above was sunshine, and all beneath was flowers; when to their clear and charmed vision this ample world was but a weedless garden, where every tint spoke nature's loveliness, and every sound breathed heaven's melody, and every breeze was but embodied fragrance; it might have been that, in this cloudless holiday love wove his roseate bondage round them, till their young hearts so grew together, a separate existence ceased, and life itself became a sweet identity."

—Anderson M. Baten, *The Philosophy of Life*, Published by Garden City Pub. Co., p. 83.

Travelers on the desert sometimes perish through exhaustion while pursuing a mirage, when they could have conserved their strength and traveled on to a life-giving spring. Beware of the fantasy of the mirage so often encountered in the area of young love.

In marriage, as in many of life's experiences, fact and fantasy, the genuine and the counterfeit are intertwined until it is difficult to distinguish. Love-stricken teenagers are romantically prone to endow each other with illusionary qualities and are deceived by veneer which to experienced eyes is most apparent. Young people should be warned against these illusions, sometimes called mirages. They should remember that before marriage each is or tries to

be at his best, but in the everyday wear and tear of married life "truth will out." Modern make-up can be made to look real and natural for a time, but it will be revealed for what it is in the "weathering" of marriage. Remember make-up will come off, hair styles will change, artificial beauty will vanish, and you must live with the residue. "Thou blind fool, love, what dost thou to mine eyes, that they behold and see not what they see." — Shakespeare

> "The whole endeavor of both parties, during the time of courtship," says Dr. Johnson, "is frequent-ly to hinder themselves from being known; to dis-guise their natural temper and real desires in hypo-critical imitation, studied compliance, and con-tinued affectation. From the time that their love was avowed, neither sees the other but in a mask; and the cheat is managed often on both sides with so much art, and discovered afterwards with so much abruptness, that each has reason to suspect that some transformation has happened, and that by a strange imposture, as in the case of Jacob, one has been courted and another married."

It is well for both boy and girl contemplating marriage to find opportunity to scratch the surface and discover what is hidden. Look for durable and permanent qualities, be not misled by camouflage. In marriage, which is life at work, the superficial is soon exposed; only the genuine can endure the hammer and chisel of married life. Young people contemplating marriage should compare notes on back-ground, family idiosyncrasies, religious convictions and activities, lifetime habits, and national peculiarities, and ask frankly, "Can we two become one?" or, speaking in terms of metals, "Are we malleable?"

To follow this analogy further, let us think of marriage as a welding process. The dictionary defines welding as "to unite closely or intimately, to join closely; to form into or as into a single piece." The average marriage, where love's fires are kept aglow, will result in a permanent weld-ing, despite, and often even assisted by the hammer blows of life. But with some metals, and some personalities, fusion is impossible. It is tragic when two hopelessly incompatible persons, on a sudden impulse, become committed to a joint lifetime project, in which others may become involuntarily involved. This can be avoided by deliberate, unhurried appraisal of available facts and by recognizing emotional fantasy for the mirage it is.

If, in comparing notes before marriage, the couple who think they are in love find irreconcilable difference of out-look, ambitions, habits, or character, then the head should take over from the heart, and, if listened to, it will counsel caution. Neither fear of hurting the other party nor timidity in the face of unpleasant duty will justify rashness. Even if the couple are engaged to be married, if they or either of them discovers irreconcilable traits, then, even though break-ing the engagement may cause embarrassment, sorrow, and heartache, it is better to cause a small wound now than to be responsible for two broken hearts later on. In other words, all who contemplate marriage should "stop, look, and listen," and then pray for wisdom to guide and courage to act.

It takes a much broader understanding than most young people have to realize that love, for all its wonders, cannot remove the irritations that are inevitable in human relation-ships, nor change the personalities of the persons involved.

Some couples fail to realize that if their marriage is to succeed they must, with eternal vigilance, keep the fragile plant of love growing by tenderly nourishing and constantly cultivating and encouraging it to unfold into full bloom.

Many young people have what they think are serious love affairs, only to find that they are fleeting and temporary. It is a tragedy when young people, while blinded or drugged by emotion, get married and then too late, meet someone whom they really love. Even among engaged couples, many break off and marry someone else and are generally grateful that they escaped the sorrow of too early and ill-considered marriage. Time should be taken for serious thought, and opportunity given for physical, mental, and spiritual maturity. Longer acquaintance will enable both to evaluate themselves and their proposed companions, to know each other's likes and dislikes, habits and dispositions, aptitudes and aspirations.

Our modern civilization increases the number of acquaintances of our young people, but in inverse ratio decreases the number they know intimately. The automobile and airplane, the telephone, the large public schools and universities, the ease with which many travel about the world —while these things make possible a slight acquaintance with a larger group, they have a tendency to encourage hair-trigger decisions, hasty and ill-considered alliances, and to make fateful promises in an atmosphere of romantic bliss.

Statistics are startling and should serve as a warning to the impetuous. Four hundred thousand divorces in the Unted States each year should emphasize the need for caution. In some states, where a three-day waiting period is required of applicants for marriage licenses, there are

thousands of couples who do not return to the license office but change their plans and marry someone else. How fortunate if the folly of these rash impulses is discovered before rather than after marriage.

Just as wise businessmen consider all the factors in a proposed partnership, so this, the most important partnership of all, a partnership which should be for time and all eternity, should be entered into only after careful and prayerful consideration and ample time in which to weigh all the factors. This is the most momentous of all life's decisions, and the contracting parties should be prepared for it and not be rushed off their feet by the blandishments of Cupid.

Too often young people mistake certain physical maturity for over-all adulthood. Too many marry when they are still entirely dependent and unprepared for the responsibilities which growing up entails. Maturity is not just a matter of calendar age nor of physical development alone. When two who contemplate joining their lives for eternity are still in the process of maturing and growing, they should check on the direction of that growth and see whether they are growing together or apart. The evolution from dependence to independence is a gradual process and requires constant adjustment as one struggles toward maturity. These growing pains are aggravated and complicated by having to adjust to another who is in similar throes.

"Only time and experience can make one fully adult." Getting married should be an ongoing or continuing process. Couples either continue to get married or begin to get unmarried. When the authorized official says "Amen" to the marriage ceremony, the young couple are not married in the

fullest sense. They have been given an opportunity to begin to get married, and this getting married process should continue throughout life. It is a process of separating facts from fantasies and learning to live with the facts. At the end of fifty years many couples are more married than they ever were before, and more truly and tenderly in love. The "twain have become one flesh," and therefore each spouse loves the other as he loves himself. Where marriage is the beginning, not the end of courtship, and where the ingredients of true courtship and love, such as kindness, courtesy, tenderness, and service are renewed and replenished, there you find an enduring home on an eternal foundation.

A bride of more than fifty years was heard to say to her seventy-six-year-old companion, "When I hear your footsteps on the sidewalk coming home in the evening, my heart begins to flutter, and I rush to the mirror to make sure I am presentable to meet my lover." Would to God that all young couples could ride the tumultuous waves, brave the storm, and continue on together until they know the joy of coming into the harbor where there is peace that "passeth understanding," and a love greater than "faith or hope."

> Grow old along with me;
> The best is yet to be,
> The last of life,
> For which the first was made.
> —Browning

Each of the partners in this relationship should recognize and respect the role assigned to his companion. The roles differ, and each person is, by nature, intended for his unique role. When the couple attempt to change places

or when either insists that the other take over the roll assigned to him, the laws of nature are violated, and there is always a penalty.

Some have said that next to self-preservation, sex instinct is the most dominant in life. In the Latter-day Saint view, the most potent motivation in human life is love. Conjugal sex experience is but one manifestation of that love. Indulgence in sex without love is lust, even within the marriage state. It is love that binds people together, causes them to seek each other's happiness before considering their own, and thus they make their own happiness complete.

True affection in marriage, which is a thing of spirit as well as body, will outlast the honeymoon and grow more beautiful with time, for it is intended to be eternal. The real glory of the married state in this life should reach its climax as the curtain falls on life's second act. (An intermediate "finis" called Death.) And then, after a brief intermission to allow one or the other of the actors to "change his costume," they will meet and continue on the eternal stage where there will be no curtain.

While marriage in the first instance is for the benefit of the contracting parties, both physical, mental, and spiritual, each must take the longer view and realize that the success or failure in this venture will carry over into the lives of posterity. When people marry they not only choose companions for life, but they also select the parents for their children and the "stock" for their posterity.

As Dr. Abraham Stone, famous marriage counselor, pointed out in a recent *Reader's Digest* article, "Mature love differs from childish love in that it desires not merely

the satisfaction of self, of one's own needs, but even more the satisfactions of the mate. A couple maturely in love, genuinely 'care' for one another. They want to establish a kinship of body and feeling. They do not romantically endow each other with illusionary qualities, but see and accept in one another both virtues and faults." Is your love mature as you choose your mate?

The person who is really and truly in love, male or female, will dedicate himself to the inspiring task of building a home and family. He would rather be with the person who is his partner in the undertaking than with anyone else in the world, be they parents, relatives, or friends. The relationship of husband and wife is the most intimate, basic and precious relationship known in life. In fact, the scriptures admonish that a man leave father and mother and cleave unto his wife.

Both parties should realize that there is no perfect person in this world and be warned against those deceptive "Isles of Eden" which exist only in the mind. Too often either the bride- or groom-to-be, or both, think they see in the other a perfection which is not really there or is colored and enlarged by rose-tinted magnifying glasses with which Cupid has supplied them.

Young people should marry someone:

Who has achieved physical, mental, emotional, and spiritual maturity.

Whom they've known long enough to appraise their "wearing qualities."

Who has achieved self-control and can love someone more than he loves himself.

Who is willing to make sacrifices for the happiness of others.

Who is willing to assume the responsibility of raising a family.

And then only if he too measures up to these standards.

O, the toils of life!
How small they seem, when love's resistless tide
Sweeps brightly o'er them! Like the scattered stones
Within a mountain streamlet, they but serve
To strike the hidden music from its flow,
And make its sparkle visible.
        —Anna Katharine Green

Why Marry Within the Church

Be ye not unequally yoked together with unbeliev-
ers.

II Cor. 6:14

Some of our young people, and others, have wondered
if the Church of Jesus Christ of Latter-day Saints is peculiar
or unique in its insistence that its members should marry
within the Church. It may be interesting to some to know
that leaders of other churches have, down through the ages,
counseled their members to marry within their own faith.

Catholic, Protestant, and Jewish leaders in all nations
agree that inter-faith marriages frequently end in separation
or divorce. Several national studies have been made on this
important question, and they show that the chances of divorce and separation are two and one-half times greater
in inter-faith marriages than where the partners are of the
same faith. These studies further show that even where
such marriages do not break up in divorce or separation, the
difference in religious opinions and convictions is at the root
of much unhappiness.

If either one or both parties to such marriages are sincere in their religious convictions, there is sure to come a
time, especially after children come into the home, when one
or the other must yield, unless both are willing to give up
religious practices altogether. If they choose the latter alternative, it means their children will be brought up without
any kind of church attachment.

Reliable statistics show that where both parents were Catholic, ninety-two percent of their sons remain Catholic. Where both parents were Protestant, sixty-eight percent of their sons were practicing Protestants, but where one parent was Catholic and the other Protestant, only thirty-four percent of the children were practicing members of either faith. There are so many adjustments to be made in the average marriage, that it is unwise to start out with fundamental differences; and differences in religion are fundamental.

Young people, during their courtship, may feel that their emotional harmony will make their differing faiths unimportant, but this does not prove to be true in actual experience. It is not difficult to maintain *friendships* across the barriers of religion, but successful marriage calls for mental, emotional, and spiritual unity, without which complete and satisfactory union between husband and wife is unattainable. Where spiritual unity pervades all phases of married life, other differences become insignificant. But antagonistic church allegiance is like a flaw in a building which extends from the foundation to the roof.

Divisive disputes caused by religious differences, generally result in conflicts in a wider area than that of specific religious belief and observance. Even if for the sake of harmony, the parties agree to become inactive in any church, still the carry-over of their early religious training, the cultural patterns and personal values, will aggravate and complicate the problems of day-to-day living.

In Orthodox Judaism there is detailed regulation in daily living. Catholicism requires submission to the authority of the church, while Protestantism generally stresses in-

dividual freedom. Most young people raised in any one of these religious groups are deeply affected by their early training, and if they marry into different faiths and under-take to raise a family, their fundamental problems are vastly increased.

In the Church of Jesus Christ of Latter-day Saints, there are many additional, fundamental reasons for marrying with-in the Church. Its members believe that the gospel of Jesus Christ has been restored, that they have a divine commission to live its principles and teach its doctrines and way of life, therefore, they cannot compromise without being untrue to themselves and to their children. Adherence to its principles and doctrines is incumbent by divine revelation up-on all its members, and they who accept such revelation are anxious that their children shall be taught its principles and live according to its standards. Some of the teachings of the Church are, by other people, looked upon as unusual and extreme. A young man or woman may, for a time, tolerate in his mate practices and indulgences which are forbidden, but the Latter-day Saint boy or girl who marries out of the Church must expect the question to arise and become more vital as children come into the home. No true Latter-day Saint would wish to have his children leave the Church, sacri-fice its blessings or be raised in another faith. By the same token, the other spouse generally would not wish to have the children raised in our Church, and here they join issue; here there is a conflict of loyalties and a parting of the ways. Again we say, religion, if sincere, is fundamental, and wis-dom would suggest in the interest of peace and happiness that not only Latter-day Saints, but men and women of other faiths, should marry members of their own church.

There is, of course, the additional incentive for LDS members to marry within the Church, and that is that only worthy members of the Church may be married in the temple. Temple marriage is for time and eternity, and children born to parents who were married in the temple belong to the parents forever. Let young men and women consider before they marry out of the Church whether they will be willing to lose their children, either here or hereafter or both, rather than overcome and reject a juvenile infatuation. They who marry out of the Church and therefore out of the temple should consider the permanence of the separation agreed to in the civil marriage ceremony, which concludes with the saddening phrase, "Until death do you part." There are, in all communities, eligible young men and women within the Church, and caution should suggest to all that they consider well the probable, and in some respects inevitable, consequences of marrying out of the Church.

Each one should try to imagine himself adjusting to the problem of seeing his or her child reared in another faith, or see the child form friendships or accept values and standards which are contrary to his own early training and deep convictions. There can be no warm family fellowship enjoyed when the parents, and later the children, differ on such essential matters. Furthermore, children raised under such conditions will themselves be inclined to minimize or disregard the importance of religion when in turn they may be seeking companions.

Thoughtful young people should, before they start dating, avoid the danger of entanglements and date only those who are of their own faith. All experienced counselors know that religious differences are among the root causes of incompatibility and unhappiness.

Some young people marry non-members in the hope that they may be converted and join the Church after marriage. It is much wiser to settle that question before marriage, and if neither one nor the other wishes to join the Church to which his fiance belongs, a broken engagement is much better than broken hearts and a broken home after the marriage ceremony. Young men and women, thinking of marriage, look forward hopefully to building peaceful, love-filled homes and raising happy, united families. If they talk to any wise marriage counselor, or the leaders of their own church or the minister of their proposed companion, they will almost invariably be advised to choose life partners whose faith and spiritual background is the same as their own.

There are enough built-in hazards in this venture without deliberately starting out with a fundamental difference. The late President Joseph F. Smith, one of the wisest and most revered of fathers, said in a general conference of the Church:

> . . . Some people feel that it does not make very much difference whether a girl marries a man in the Church, full of the faith of the gospel, or an unbeliever. Some of our young people have married outside the Church, but very few of those who have done it have failed to come to grief. I would like to see Latter-day Saint women marry Latter-day Saint men, and Latter-day Saint men marry Latter-day Saint women; and let Methodists marry Methodists, Catholics marry Catholics, and Presbyterians marry Presbyterians, and so on to the limit. Let them keep within the pale of their own faith and church, and marry and inter-marry there, and let the Latter-day Saints do the same thing in their Church; . . .   —Oct. C.R. 1909, pp. 5, 6

We receive many letters from people who face divorce and its attendant evils as a direct consequence of their having disregarded the above counsel. The following is typical:

Dear Elder:

As I listened to your address today, I wished, so deep in my heart, that I had listened to similar advice ten years ago. At the age of 22 I married a non-Mormon. I had dated good Mormon boys, but, although I had respect for them, they had failed to "sweep me off my feet." . . .

The time has come when my duty is first to my children. We can no longer spend our Sundays hunting or visiting. My children *need* to go to church. My husband is willing that I should take them, but I must go *alone*. We are separated in the one thing that could bring us the most joy. (Worshipping as a family.)

I can see my marriage slowly slipping away from me. Our central interests are different. He likes dogs and sports, mine must be church and children. I must take the children slowly to me and away from him. We have no common ground on which to meet in time of trial and need. Couples who cannot pray together, can seldom *talk* to each other. The loneliness I feel these days is almost more than I can bear. The worst part of the whole situation is the *conflicts* with yourself, knowing that your duty is to the children and the Church, and yet *wanting* the companionship of your husband. I sincerely hope you will continue to impress these important facts on our youth. I don't believe this subject can be stressed too much to our young boys and girls. May God be with me, that I may find a solution to my problem. I sincerely hope He can help me do the best with the mistake I have made.

There are, of course, many good, sincere, devoted people in other churches. Our objection to marrying them stems, not from any "Holier-than-thou" feeling, but from a desire that both parties avoid the unhappiness which experience shows is almost inevitable. We would advise any Catholic, Protestant, or Jew not to marry a Latter-day Saint and for the same reasons. Marriage is, to Latter-day Saints, not only the most serious and important of life's adventures, but it is, when properly solemnized, the gateway into the kingdom of heaven. Furthermore, it is prerequisite to admittance to the highest degree of the celestial kingdom. Be satisfied with nothing less than CELESTIAL MARRIAGE.

II. Prerequisites — Education for Marriage

Foundation Stones

Therefore whosoever heareth these sayings of mine, and doeth them, I will liken him unto a wise man, which built his house upon a rock:

And the rain descended, and the floods came, and the winds blew, and beat upon that house; and it fell not: for it was founded upon a rock.

—Matthew 7:24-25

Someone asks, when should we start to train young people for happy married life, and the answer is, "Preparation should begin before they are born, i.e., with the grandparents and parents, or at latest while the parents-to-be are themselves little children."

The way married couples meet and cope with life's problems, and with each other's weaknesses, idiosyncrasies, and foibles, will determine in large measure how their own children will solve the age-old and continuing problems of human relationships. Among these human relationships marriage is the most intimate, most delicate, may be the most beautiful, and is sometimes the most fragile.

At the time of marriage, or even before, each couple should decide whether they wish their children, when they marry, to remember homes in which there were love, loyalty, peace, and happiness, or incompatibility, contention, strife, and misery. The answer to this question depends upon the character, personalities, integrity, and constancy of the couple themselves, for in their home some future brides and

grooms are to spend the most impressionable years of their lives.

Children carry with them into their future homes the effects of the daily atmosphere which pervaded the homes of their youth. If the homes of their childhood were happy and harmonious, filled with love, kindness, tenderness, loyalty, and laughter, they will strive to establish similar homes of their own. The seeds of success or failure in marriage are often sown in the homes of the parents of the young people who are to be the brides and grooms of the future.

The experiences of young people in their own homes have much to do with their thought patterns concerning marriage. They note but may not mention the attitudes of parents toward each other and sometimes accept as normal that which in undesirable. These thought patterns carry over into later life, and when they themselves are married, these early memories are reflected in the success or failure of their own marriage.

The boy or girl who has a happy childhood will look forward to continuing happiness in marriage and will unconsciously adopt many of the methods and attitudes of the parents toward each other and toward their children. On the other hand the child who has no happy memories of home and childhood is liable to consider unhappiness a normal condition of life and be resigned to it as part of the so-called curse which Adam brought upon the world.

But in addition to the atmosphere of the home in which the children are raised, there should be forthright, frank, and persistent pre-marital instruction by the parents, and, when needed, by church officials, teachers, and counselors. The success and permanence of new families is or

should be the concern of all segments of our society, as the family relationship is the keystone to our whole system of both church and state.

Too many of our young people get married recklessly either to get away from unhappy homes or as an exciting experiment, with very little knowledge of the world or of human relationships, except the often garbled and distorted impressions gained from picture shows, radio and television plays, or from cheap fiction.

The Church has a grave responsibility in this field, and while much is being done by way of advice, admonition, and counsel through Church oganizations, the ever-increasing divorce rate, resulting partly from the lowering of minimum marriage age is a constant concern of Church leaders and is creating a problem which strikes at the very root of our civilization.

The responsibility of training our young people for the most challenging, most beautiful, and potentially the most permanent and rewarding of all human relationships, rests primarily with the parents.

Too many parents avoid this responsibility, some aspects of which are sometimes thought to be too delicate for frank discussion. In some case the discussion of sex is entirely taboo. The fact is, there is no area of human experience, development, and education more necessary, more vital —but more neglected—than is the field of preparation for marriage in all its aspects. In its psychological, emotional, and spiritual phases, marriage, in the life of individuals, is one of the supreme tests of character. This is and has been true at all times, in every culture and under the widest variety of circumstances.

Dr. Mortimer J. Adler, editor-in-chief of the Syntopicon of Great Books of the Western World, says: "The relation between men and women in and out of marriage, the relation of husband and wife before and after marriage, the relation of parents and children—these create crises and tensions, conflicts between love and duty, between reason and the passions, from which no individual can entirely escape. Marriage is not only a typically human problem but it is the one problem which both psychologically and morally touches every man, woman and child. Sometimes the resolution is tragic, sometimes the outcome seems to be happy, almost blessed, but whether the human life is built on this foundation or broken against these rocks, it is violently shaken in the process and forever shaped."

While it is inspiring to note the high hopes and great expectations of young couples as they approach the marriage altar, sometimes we older folk are a bit frightened and deeply concerned when we consult statistics. Each young couple is liable to say, as they start together on this journey through eternity, "There never was a marriage like ours," and that may be true, but it may take thirty, forty, or fifty years to prove it.

A successful marriage cannot be bought in ready-to-wear stores. Each must be tailored to fit the individuals and must be kept up-to-date by such alterations and changes as life's "wear and tear" may require. There must be occasional refitting into the changing patterns as life progresses.

We cannot over-emphasize the beauty, sanctity, responsibility, and the divinely intended permanence of the marriage covenant. It is not and must not be a temporary venture, begun with the idea that at the first appearance

of difficulty a release will be sought in the divorce courts. All should be reminded that the effects of this venture carry over into the lives of posterity, and even into eternity.

In the Church we are constantly reminded that successful marriage results from sharing and solving problems and common experiences, from making adjustments and sacrifices, from prayer and worship together. The divine purpose and final goal of married life is immortality and eternal lives. If this goal is kept in mind, love and marriage take on a spiritual and eternal quality and may become so enduring as to defy the grave and rob death of its victory.

Someone has said: "Problems are the things we see when we take our eyes off our goal." They who keep their "mind's eye" upon the goal of immortality, eternal life and eternal increase will not be daunted by the daily problems and vexations of life.

The sensible couple or family who start on a trip in an automobile, whether on business or pleasure, with a promise of something valuable or worthwhile at the end of the journey, will not be deterred or thrown into panic if something goes wrong with the car. They stop and fix it or take it to a garage. If a new part is needed, which cannot be obtained at the service station or small town en route, and a layover is required while the garage man obtains and installs a new part, they, if they are wise and well adjusted, will make good use of the enforced rest. Without recriminations or worry, they will see the sights of the area, get acquainted with some of the people, go to a show, and, in various ways, turn what might have been a tragedy into a holiday and enrich the trip for all. They continue on and win the reward.

If something goes wrong in the home, or if there is a storm of quarreling, caused by tensions and triggered by temper, why not be as wise and sane here as on an auto, mobile trip. Why not relax, go for a walk, chop some wood, whip up a cake, get some recreation, and let the storm blow over as all storms do? Unfortunately, some couples, in such situations, figuratively set fire to the car and walk off in opposite directions into the desert, without regard for the welfare of other members of the family, and convert what was a minor matter to an irreparable tragedy. Oh, that married people would grow up and "act their age!"

The necessity for pre-marital counseling with religious leaders, practicing physicians and professional counselors, *all supplemental to the primary responsibility of the parents,* in other words, the importance of laying a solid foundation, is being recognized by leaders of our society. Such counsel ing, education, and training is a vital and necessary part of the training of youth for the responsibilities and blessings of life both here and hereafter. Such training, sanctified by practical religion in the home, will help young people to approach this all-important phase of life as a sacred and solemn venture where, if both are true to their covenants, real love for each other will continue to grow whatever the vicissitudes of life.

Frederick W. Robertson wrote the following concise comment which we think will provoke thought:

Marriage is not a union, merely between two creatures — it is a union between two spirits; and the intention of that bond is to perfect the nature of both, by supplementing their deficiencies with the force of contrast, giving to each sex those ex-

cellences in which it is naturally deficient; to the one, strength of character and firmness of moral will; to the other, sympathy, meekness, tenderness; and just so solemn and glorious as these ends are for which the union was intended, just so terrible are the consequences if it be perverted and abused; for there is no earthly relationship which has so much power to ennoble and to exalt. There are two rocks, in this world of ours, on which the soul must either anchor or be wrecked — the one is God, and the other is the sex opposite.

—Frederick W. Robertson (1816-53)
English divine

Emotional Maturity

I do not ask for any crown
But that which all may win;
Nor try to conquer any world
Except the one within.
Be thou my guide until I find,
Led by a tender hand,
The happy kingdom in myself
And dare to take command.

—Louisa May Alcott

The need for emotional equilibrium in married life becomes more apparent to the marriage counselor with each day's assortment of interviews with husbands and wives who are seeking help and counsel. Even among older couples who have lived together many years, we find that one or neither has ever grown up emotionally.

We frequenty find that people who are having marital problems are so close to the problem that they do not recognize it for what it is. Normal and reasonable people, in case of a sprained ankle or broken arm, will seek immediate treatment and relief, but they fail to realize that as much sorrow and unhappiness derive from emotional problems as from physical handicaps. Frequently the output of emotional energy greatly exceeds the intake, and this results inevitably, if not reversed, in emotional bankruptcy.

The man who "flies off the handle" when his wife asks him to do some small chore about the house, who

becomes indignant and "bawls her out," or who pouts and sulks over petty things, is still an infant emotionally.

We who meet hundreds of such cases find that fre' quently the explosion which brought them to the office resulted from an undetected or unrecognized accumulation of irritations, indignation, frustration, and confusion, all building up into a final conflagration, sparked by an unruly tongue.

> Anger blows out the lamp of the mind. In the examination of a great and important question, every one should be serene, slow'pulsed, and calm.
>   —Ingersoll

Men and women should ask themselves occasionally, "Am I not intelligent enough and mature enough to handle these little irritations in a sensible manner?" Surely most adults can handle small or even large problems if taken one at a time and disposed of without allowing them to accumu' late. Some people seem to get great satisfaction out of "digging up the past," "rehashing old grievances," and plac' ing all the blame on the spouse.

Marriage, like life, is made up of small matters, and one's reaction to them and handling of them determines whether the marriage is to be a success or failure.

We hear quite frequently of the nagging wife and certainly when we find her we find a real problem, but there are also nagging husbands, though they may not be so widely advertised. The husband who makes an emotional problem out of small defects in home management on the part of the wife, who alternately scolds and sulks and threatens, for example, over the size of the telephone or electric light bill, who threatens to take out the phone

or disconnect the light, should stop and figure up the actual cost and compare it with some of his own extravagances. The balance will often be in favor of the wife.

Also, the nagging husband is liable to overemphasize and exaggerate little oversights on the part of his wife and treat them as though they were matters of life and death. How often a husband is heard to say, "You *never* have meals on time. You *always* forget to have my shirts ready. You *never* realize that I am tired." Surely there have been exceptions to the above universals, and the husband himself, perhaps, was guilty of the very things of which he accused his spouse — like the father who said to his son, "I have told you *a million times* not to exaggerate."

In an excellent book on this subject written by Dr. Roy Burkhardt, entitled *From Friendship to Marriage,* published by Harper and Brothers, New York, 1938, the author asked a thousand wives what they thought were the marks of a good husband. From the replies we quote the following:

He is not bored to stay home in the evening.
He never reminds me of what a good cook his mother is.
He helps with the dishes.
He enjoys reading good books with me.
He tells me interesting things about his work.
He notices little changes I make in the home.
He always cleans the tub or basin after washing.
He appreciates the new dishes I prepare.
He knows how to pull me out of the dumps.

Not all of the above may be called trivial things. They and a thousand more like them — and a similar list might be made of the marks of a good wife — are the little

things that each spouse should watch for and practice. After all, married life, if it is to be successful, requires study and practice and correcting one's faults. Competence in any field results from practice and experience, whether it be science or art, music or drama, law or medicine, or, in another field, whether it be golf, football, swimming, fighting—all require study and practice and correcting one's faults.

By permission I quote a page from Dr. Paul Popenoe's book *Marriage Is What You Make it*.

> Study and practice, study and practice — those are the things that help a man to be a good husband. How is it that they ignore the fact. Let Mr. J. serve as an illustration. He has just taken up golf.
>
> "I'm glad you learned golf," I assured him, "It must be . . ."
>
> "I said I was just beginning."
>
> "Well, lots of other people play success-fully," I replied. "It's a well-known game and you have read about it, even watched people play. You certainly don't think that you are unable to start out and immediately go along with the best of them."
>
> "I don't see the joke," he replied sourly.
>
> "Come to think of it, I believe you're right," I replied. "You don't expect to start golf and, without study or practice, play a perfect game. . ."
>
> "What's the point of all this, Dr. Popenoe?"
>
> "Merely that you are proceeding intelligently in golf, knowing that you need years of study and practice to make a good showing; and yet you come to me to complain that you can't get along

in marriage — which is certainly no less important and no less difficult than golf — and it appears that you plan neither to study nor to practice, and yet assume that you should be able to play a perfect game from the first day."

He looked at me sullenly.

"I was reminded of this, just before you came in," I continued, "by some remarks which Leland E. Hinsie, professor of psychiatry at Columbia University makes in this book. . ."

"You think I need a psychiatrist," Mr. J. muttered.

I started to read from the book: "In just what other department of living do we expect to jump overnight from inexperience to experience. . ."

"The wedding night," Mr. J. remarked, with a faint grin for the first time.

"Nor do we gain eminence quickly in avocations," I continued to read. "We allow years for the achievement of a position of soundness in music, the theater, travel, and so on."

He started to interrupt but I continued reading: "If we gave as little time to the training of our intellect as we do to our emotions, very few would rise above the level of idiocy."

And later in the same book he quotes the confession of a husband, who, after an interview, said:

"I can see that I have been running the family a little highhandedly. The children were small, my wife busy, and it was too easy for me to be a little dictator, to order everybody around just as I used to do in the army from the supreme elevation of my position as top sergeant."

While many of the causes of marital failure are biological, emotional immaturity is detected in a large number of cases that come to the marriage counselor for help and possible solution.

Each person has many adjustments to make as he struggles toward maturity, and these growing pains should not be complicated by having to adjust to another who is in similar throes. Youth as well as age is a kind of infirmity. Only time and experience can make one wholly adult.

After marriage little misunderstandings, if not talked out and thrown out, may lead to tragedy. Anything that tends to irritate, aggravate, or alienate the companions in this holy relationship, should be discovered, acknowledged, and removed before real tragedy occurs. A pebble in the shoe, though very small, if not removed, may irritate, fester and even poison the foot; thus may small irritations and disputes, if unresolved, lead to serious consequences.

Some whose marriages have gone on the rocks cynically say, "Marriage should be spelled mirage." This, of course, is only a self-justifying excuse unless there has been intentional deceit. Neither should ask nor expect perfection in the other for the simple reason that he cannot give what he asks. True love is not blind, but it has the genius to magnify virtues and minimize faults when looking at the beloved.

> When I was a child, I spake as a child, I under
> stood as a child I thought as a child: but when
> I became a man, I put away childish things.
>
> I Corinthians 13:11

Modesty, the Hallmark of a Lady

Mutual respect and consideration are, next to fidelity and love, the most important stones in the foundation of a happy home. Self-respect is prerequisite to being respected by others. We are all judged and classified by appearance and conduct.

In our youth conferences, Gold and Green balls, and supervised sports, the modest and attractive attire of our young women has elicited the praise and admiration of visitors in all lands where these distinctive LDS functions are held.

Most of our girls are innately modest in dress, speech, and conduct. Most of them still blush at any accidental exposure and resent any unseemly or suggestive conversation. Certainly few of them are ever guilty of intentional immodesty or of unladylike speech or conduct.

We honor and respect our cultured and refined young ladies and are grateful to them for upholding the high standards of true ladylike conduct which distinguished their mothers and grandmothers despite the rugged pioneer conditions in which they lived.

We have no nostalgic yearning for "the good old days." They had their time and place and we appreciate the distinctive examples of our fathers and mothers who met life's problems with notable success. Though the poet said, "Time makes ancient good uncouth," our ancestors had some values,

standards, and fashions which were based on discriminating good sense, deep spiritual insight, and religious faith. These values do not change with time.

We commend the youth of the Church for upholding its standards and ideals as set forth by the Prophet Joseph Smith in the Articles of Faith:

> We believe in being honest, true, chaste, benevolent, virtuous and in doing good to all men; indeed, we may say that we follow the admonition of Paul—We believe all things, we hope all things, we have endured many things, and hope to be able to endure all things. If there is anything virtuous, lovely, or of good report, or praiseworthy, we seek after these things.

We deplore and denounce any fad or fashion which waters down or makes insipid these soul-saving principles of truth and idealism.

The young women who wish to establish happy and enduring homes will resist the down-drag of the subtle vices of pretense, vanity, and impropriety. They should seek the companionship of and emulate those who are modest, refined, cultured, and respected. Modern styles and social customs sometimes lure our young people into unsuspected and undesirable habits of speech and dress.

We wonder if our girls know what kind of females they imitate when they immodestly expose their bodies to public view because it may be fashionable. They should know of the lewd, sinister, and sensuous designs of such females in these disgusting displays. If they knew the source of some modern fashions, no sensible, self-respecting girl

would mimic their authors or risk the implications and deductions of immodest exposure and conduct.

Also, if young women knew how good men, young and old, react to such exposures, we doubt if they would be so foolish and naive. The immodest revealing of the female form causes the lewd to leer and lust, decent men to blush and protest, while brothers and fathers are embar- rassed, offended, and alarmed. Even lewd men have a certain disgust for nude women.

The exposing of the uncovered body to public view is like a "for sale" notice indicating "cheap, shopworn, or marked-down goods." In a mercantile establishment, such merchandise generally invites handling and is cheapened and soiled thereby.

Decent men looking for wives and choosing mothers for their children, reject the girls who make a public display of their bodies. They want wives who will become exem- plars to their own daughters, and they know immodesty is the first step toward unchastity. Modesty indicates moral integrity which is respected by decent people everywhere. All true gentlemen honor and revere modest virgins and saintly mothers. God himself sanctified and glorified both virginity and motherhood when he made them the vehicle for the mortal advent of His Son. Also the Lord, through His prophets, designated the body as the temple in which the Holy Spirit may dwell. Any immodesty inducing or causing others to have licentious thoughts is desecration of that holy temple. Can you imagine an immodest Madonna?

We men would prefer that women do not imitate us in dress or manners. We admire femininity and protest against anything that makes women appear masculine or

manlike — it detracts from their beauty. It is obvious that the more a girl looks like a boy the less she looks like a lady. God made you different from us, and we prefer to have you keep your place on the exalted pedestal of potential or actual motherhood. When hiking, horseback riding or in certain sports, trousers for women may be permitted, but wearing tight, ill-fitting, and form-emphasizing slacks, shorts, or sweaters, on the streets or in public places is not in good taste. Shorts and "halters" are disgusting in any public place, and yet these ugly semi-coverings have gone from short and snug to shorter and tighter until modesty is dethroned.

A tourist mother and daughter were recently seen in a shoe store, both in short shorts. They sat down and waited to be served. There were two available male clerks, but neither appeared to notice them. The manager also observed the waiting females and allowed them to leave the store without being served. He commended his clerks for having the modesty which the women lacked.

But it is not the *young* women only who offend in this respect. Some who are middle aged and buxom, older but not more decorous, look as if they had been poured, molten-like, into so-called "slacks" or revealing shorts or sweaters. Such people should be provided with portable four-way mirrors so they could "see themselves as others see them" and be covered at least with shame. Simple decency calls for a little good sense in dress and for privacy when semi-undressed.

The demands of modesty and decency extend beyond dress and appearance. Immodest, profane, or vulgar speech, which leads so often to improper conduct, is always rep-

rehensible. Telling or even listening to unclean stories is like contaminating the air or voluntarily inhaling germ-laden gas. They who are guilty of this offense are usually seeking to get attention by making people laugh and thus become the "life of the party." They seem to forget that nothing foul is funny and that though they for the moment "have the floor" many of their captive listeners are offended and digusted and they themselves listed as socially repugnant.

The man or woman who is guilty of profanity, swear-ing, or crude slang unwittingly reveals a soiled mind and a limited vocabularly and is pitied and shunned by all cul-tured people. Profaning the name of God is an affront to Him, and He has forbidden it.

We pray that virtue and modesty may garnish the thoughts and adorn the lives of our people, young and old; that we may be known for our temperance, propriety, cul-ture, and integrity. Let our thoughts, words, dress, and general deportment indicate our belief in the sanctity of the body as the temple of God even as Paul declared it to be:

> . . . for ye are the temple of the living God; as God hath said, I will dwell in them, and walk in them; and I will be their God, and they shall be my people.
>
> —II Cor. 6:16

> If any man defile the temple of God, him shall God destroy; for the temple of God is holy, *which temple ye are.*
>
> I Cor. 3:17 (italics added)

To defile is to tarnish and to tarnish is "to destroy the luster of as by exposure." Young ladies, be ladies under all circumstances and proudly wear the Hallmark of Modesty.

Purity Is Priceless

My strength is as the strength of ten, because my
heart is pure.

—Tennyson

Who shall ascend into the hill of the Lord? or who
shall stand in his holy place?
He that hath clean hands, and a pure heart: . . .

—Psalm 24:3-4

The richest diadem in all the world is worn only by the
pure in heart. It is a priceless jewel, a gift from heaven bestowed on all at birth. In life's crucible it is smelted, bur-
nished, made to sparkle, and its worth is enhanced by time.
Though it is fragile it should not be kept in a glass showcase
like the crown jewels. Its value is increased by wearing.
There is a distinction between innocence and purity. One is
passive and the other active. Someone has paraphrased one
of Ella Wheeler Wilcox's poems as follows:

> It's easy enough to be virtuous
>   When nothing tempts you to stray,
> When without and within no voice of sin
>   Is luring your soul away;
> But it's only a negative virtue
>   Until it is tried by fire.
> And the soul that is worth the blessings of earth
>   Is the soul that resists desire.

Life is crammed with risk and danger but despite this
we all rejoiced at the prospect of earth life. In fact, one purpose of life is that we might develop physical, mental, and

spiritual strength through struggle. If there is to be growth there must be activity. We must push back the boundaries which hem us in, and this means ever-increasing and widening contact with life and with people.

Hardy plants grow in the open garden, where there are wind and rain and occasional frost. Products of the hot house—plants or people—are usually weak and puny. The person who is timid, passive, and negative as a result of over-solicitude and sheltering, may be, in a sense, innocent, but his untried virtues will be too fragile to endure life's tests. Of course, no one will deliberately court temptation. The very appearance of evil should be shunned and avoided, but no free person can reach maturity without meeting it; therefore, if we are to keep unsullied, we must develop an active and sturdy type purity which can keep itself unspotted and uncontaminated, even in an environment or atmosphere which, without resistance, would debase it. As it is possible for a lily to grow in a swamp and keep its whiteness, so one can keep his life pure and holy, even in the midst of worldliness and pleasure-loving associations. If man's virtue is positive, he can, like the Gulf Stream, carry his influence far out into the ocean and modify the climate for miles around.

Each person should revere and honor the sanctity of life, and live on the high plateau where self-respect is paramount. This he will do if he remembers that his life proceeds from God. No fleeting gratification can compensate its loss. Young men and women contemplating marriage should keep their lives sweet and pure, wholesome and invincible, not only that they themselves may have the deep satisfaction of maintaining self-esteem, but also that they may transmit to those who follow them the priceless heritage of innate purity.

This "strength of ten" gives confidence to youth and benediction to the aged. All find delight in the companionship of those whose thoughts, conversation, and conduct are immaculate.

The story is told that some shepherds once saw an eagle soar out from a crag. It flew majestically far up into the sky but by and by became unsteady and began to waver in its flight. At length one wing dropped and then the other, and the poor bird fell swiftly to the ground. The shepherds sought the fallen bird and found that a little serpent had fastened itself upon it while it was resting upon the crag. The eagle did not know that the serpent was there, but it crawled through the feathers and while the proud monarch was sweeping through the air, its fangs were thrust into the eagle's flesh, and he came reeling into dust. This could be the story of many a life. Some secret sin has been eating its way into the heart and at last a proud life lies soiled and dishonored in the dust.

Jeremy Taylor lists some of the progeny of purity as follows: "A pure mind in a chaste body is the mother of wisdom and deliberation, sober counsels and ingenious action, open deportment and sweet carriage, sincere principles and unprejudicate understanding, love of God and self-denial, peace and confidence, holy prayers and spiritual comfort, and the pleasure of spirit infinitely greater than the sottish pleasure of unchastity."

When virile, ambitious young men—and we meet many of them—wear the badge of purity with the grace and comeliness of a virgin, we see evidence of man's innate Godlike status. God requires purity in men as well as women. We can establish a virtuous society only when both men and women keep morally clean. The righteous man is invincible.

We wish the law could compel the authors of salacious and pornographic books, indecent movies, and suggestive TV shows to blazen across all such productions, in flaming words, the warning, "Unclean—Unclean." This was the warning that the lepers were required to shout out in Eastern countries when anyone not so cursed approached them. Let our young men and women avoid contact with leprous innuendos, unclean thoughts or words, or actions, or anything that might deprive them of the priceless gem of purity. The various media of public communication often give the false impression that love is physical attraction alone.

We urge our young men and women to be on guard against even the idea or suggestion of indecency, for ideas are like mustard seeds, small at first but capable of phenomenal growth. Even the shadow of evil might leave some soil upon the unsullied whiteness of the virgin mind.

A chief of police recently said he could rid the jails of two-thirds of the boy criminals in a year if he could banish bad plays from our theaters and put bad books out of print.

Even they who make no professions of moral decency have great respect for and sometimes envy those who live a righteous life.

During the war, two officers in London were walking between Piccadilly and Leicester Square. One was an admitted "rounder" and the other a Latter-day Saint. They were accosted by some girls of the underworld. The officer said, "I'll go with one of you, but this man won't because he is a Mormon." The Mormon officer went to his hotel room alone and retired. Later in the night the other man came in and told of his riotous time. The Mormon officer, in an

attempt to discover what was underneath the rough exterior of his friend, facetiously said to him, calling him by name, "In the future, when we are out together, let me make my own decisions. Sometime I might decide to have a night of revelry myself." Whereupon the other officer turned on him, and swearing, said, "........, ..., if I thought you meant that I think I'd want to kill you. You are the only man I know who has kept his life unsullied. You possess that which is above all price. That which you have is of more value and gives more deep satisfaction than a thousand nights of debauchery. You're on a lonely pedestal, but for God's sake and your own stay there."

The man whose heart is pure is invincible. His integrity is his shield and virtue is his armor. He will be impervious to slander, envy, hatred, or malice, and they who seek to injure him will bring ignominy upon themselves.

The righteous man has nothing to hide. He is not afraid of the sunlight. He does not live in the fear that "truth will out." He has done nothing of which he need be ashamed, and is therefore fearless. But let him wear his distinction with humility and boast not of his virtue, for in this field as in others pride goeth before a fall.

Quoting from President David O. McKay:

But there is a beauty every girl has—a gift from God, as pure as the sunlight, and as sacred as life. It is a beauty that all men love, a virtue that wins all men's souls. That beauty is chastity. Chastity without skin beauty may enkindle the soul; skin beauty without chastity can kindle only the eye. Chastity enshrined in the mold of true womanhood will hold true love eternally.

The flower by the roadside that catches the dust of every traveler is not the one to be admired and is seldom if ever plucked; but the one blooming away up on the hillside, protected by a perpendicular cliff is the flower with the virgin perfume, the one the boy will almost risk his life to possess.

Gospel Ideals, pp. 450, 451

Yes, purity is priceless. God gave it to you at birth with a charge that you keep it unsullied. Should you meet an enemy who demands: "Your honor or your life" — keep your honor for "both grow in one, take honor from me, and my life is done."

Dignifying or Debasing Sex

So spake the cherub, and his grave rebuke,
Severe in youthful beauty, added grace
Invincible: abashed the devil stood,
And felt how awful goodness is.
                                        —Milton

In our system of education of youth in family, school, and church, we often neglect one phase of growing up, one essential discipline. We, of course, have high school and college courses on physical hygiene, biology, genetics, etc., but the spiritual and religious significance of the sex aspects of their development should be impressed upon the youth.

Many marriages have been wrecked on the dangerous rocks of ignorant and debased sex behavior, both before and after marriage. Gross ignorance on the part of newly-weds on the subject of the proper place and functioning of sex results in much unhappiness and many broken homes.

Thousands of young people come to the marriage altar almost illiterate insofar as this basic and fundamental function is concerned. The sex instinct is not something which we need to fear or be ashamed of. It is God-given and has a high and holy purpose. Through the union of the sexes God provided for the perpetuity of the race. Reproduction is a law pervading nature everywhere. Through the operation of this divine law God's creative work continues. But the sex instinct is not, as some have claimed, the strongest urge in life. When compared with the urge for food and for

security, it is relatively weak. We would not, however, underestimate its power for good or ill.

Our homes and society are responsible for lack of education in this field. The family is the place, of course, where wise and progressive instruction on this subject should be given. Help is sometimes given by the school and the church, but many teachers are not qualified and therefore shy away from so intimate a subject. As this powerful and insistent urge develops, it must be intelligently controlled and disciplined. It is here that the young person encounters the bewildering crosscurrents of his biological, physiological, and psychological nature. With a healthy and informed mind and with a proper understanding of the spiritual significance of his nature and his life, the young person can harness and employ this tremendous force as he drives toward immortality and eternal life.

Some sound instruction in this area will help a man to realize the numberless, delicate differentiations and modifications in the life and reactions of the normal woman. There are many first-class doctors, who are also fathers, to whom young men could go for information and instruction. But fundamentally, in addition to all that can be learned from others, he must teach himself moderation, self-control, and tender consideration.

One of the cornerstones of happy married life, so often disregarded by parents as they train their children for future wedlock, is the necessity for harmonious sexual activities between the parties thereto. Each couple should, with reverence, intelligence, and consideration, build solidly and skilfully on this stone in the foundation of the temple of the home. The man who seeks physiological or biological satis-

faction without regard to the effects of his conduct on the highly sensitive, physical, mental, and spiritual personality of his wife, fails to realize how fundamental proper sex behavior is to future happiness and preserving the home.

The reprehensible misuse of such media as radio, television, picture shows, and magazines, has tended to excite an unwholesome, distorted, and even morbid interest in this subject. Suggestive and often indecent pictures and, more recently, disgusting pornographic pamphlets have stirred the curiosity of youth who are encouraged or induced to experiment and experience, and this is leading to widespread promiscuity.

Great cities of ancient times, and more modern Greece and Rome, were brought to rubble heaps and their civilizations destroyed because of the overemphasis and perversion of the sex instinct. Commercialized vice and sexual promiscuity are striking hammer blows at the rock foundation of our homes and of our society. Attempts to control this fundamental urge by external restraints alone have generally been unsuccessful. Education should precede attempted regulation.

Every normal person is equipped with a sex urge. Its misuse or promiscuous expression brings sorrow, heartbreak, disease, and death, and if this urge is not regulated or checked, our civilization must crumble as have others.

Ignorance and blundering on the part of newlyweds account in large measure for the fact that one out of three marriages end in divorce. Our young people should avoid the various vulgar approaches to this essentially delicate, beautiful, and Godlike capacity.

We want our young people to know that sex is not an unmentionable human misfortune, and certainly it should not be regarded as a sordid but necessary part of marriage. There is no excuse for approaching this most intimate relationship in life without true knowledge of its meaning and its high purpose. This is an urge which more insistently than others calls for self-control and intelligence. The young man who practices self-control, especially during the honeymoon will reap rich rewards in after years. He will win the deep and abiding respect of his wife, which is indispensable to lasting love and will establish a beautiful relationship for all the years to come.

Some shortsighted persons claim that what they do to themselves or between themselves is no one's business but their own, but young people contemplating marriage and young married couples too must know that improper sex conduct is not a private affair and that many innocent people may be seriously affected. The young married couple should make sure that the children who come into their home have proper emotional patterns, habits, and training to guide them.

Unwise and unrestrained sex conduct can destroy love, which, if nurtured, protected, and kept sweet can and should unfold its highest potentialities of joy, dignity, and moral value in the marriage state.

When lovers celebrate their marriage ceremony, they join in sacred covenants; not alone because of ecclesiastical pronouncements are they sacred, but they are and should also be sacred because human life is sacred, and they stand at the very fountain of human life, which they must not desecrate.

If the bride and groom, as they kneel at the altar, love each other ardently with spirit as well as senses, and if each is wise enough to keep that love aglow, then it is difficult to imagine a situation which would tempt them to violate their covenants with each other and with those yet unborn, for whom they will be responsible.

When the Lord established marriage—and He is its author—He made sex union lawful within that relationship, and it becomes both honorable and sanctified. But extramarital sexual indulgence is a debasing sin. Sex immorality leads to or is compounded of many other offenses against God and man.

Young people should know that, generally speaking, people do not lose their virtue by one impulsive act, but they descend a step at a time. They who are guilty of immodesty, necking, petting, and other secret and unwholesome practices, should know that they are on the very brink of sorrow and disgrace. They are, voluntarily, being led by the deceiver of men's souls down the path of misery and shame.

There are various types and degrees of infidelity, lewdness, and licentiousness, various ways in which men and women tempt themselves or permit themselves to be tempted to commit adultery, and Lucifer uses all of them, even the secret thoughts of the mind and unclean conversation as weapons in his arsenal to destroy mankind.

The late President Joseph F. Smith, the sixth President of the Church, and a prophet of God, spoke out emphatically on this universal evil. In *Gospel Doctrine,* page 275-276, we read, "Though often regarded as insignificant by those not knowing the will of God, they (sexual sins) are in His eyes

an abomination, and if we are to remain His favorite people, they must be shunned as the gates of Hell. The evil results of these sins are so patent in vice, crime, misery, and disease, that it would appear that all, young and old, must perceive and sense them. They are destroying the world. If we are to be preserved we must abhor them, shun them, not practice the least of them, for they weaken and enervate, they kill men spiritually, they make him unfit for the company of the righteous and the presence of God."

And again President Smith wrote in *The Improvement Era,* vol. 20, page 739, "No more loathsome cancer disfigures the body and soul of society today than the frightful affliction of sexual sin. It vitiates the very foundation of life and bequeaths its foul effects to the yet unborn as a legacy of death. It lurks in hamlet and city, in mansion and the hovel, as a ravening beast it waits for prey and it sulks through the land in blasphemous defiance of the laws of God and of man."

This chapter is written on this important subject and included in this little book on marriage as a warning to all young people who may read to be on guard against the insidious and sometimes blatant blandishments of Satan. The seeds of wreckage and destruction of marriage, home, and family may be sown by thoughtless or wilful conduct in early youth, sometimes lured on by the deceiving whisper, "No one will ever know." Even if that were true, and it is as false as are all of Satan's promises, still the guilty one himself, through loss of self-respect, will have paid a price far beyond any value or reward which Lucifer may promise.

Someone, whose name I do not know, wrote the following challenging statement, "If you would be among the

noble you must be noble. If you would be among the wise you must be wise. If you would be among the pure in heart, you must be pure in heart." The password to these select groups is, "Are you worthy?" You may get by by falsifying, but if you do, you will have to suffer the misery of seeing your own mediocrity unmasked in the presence of greatness.

Wickedness Never Was Happiness

Some have wondered why the Church considers the sin of unchastity a cardinal sin. There are many reasons for considering it so serious, one of which is the effect upon the sinner himself. He who is morally unclean sins against himself. No one can sin and really feel good about it. Some part of him constantly protests, and he is therefore at war with himself, and war is always destructive. One may do a kindly act such as visiting the sick, feeding the hungry, assisting those in trouble, and experience a joy and satisfaction in which his whole being participates. There are no aftereffects of remorse, fear of detection, regret, desire to escape, avoidance of erstwhile comrades. But there is no greater tragedy than the perversion and degradation of love. Wickedness never was happiness.

In a Judaeo-Christian society founded on revelation from God, intimate relations between men and women must be reserved exclusively for marriage. That this is the will of God is proclaimed in both Old and New Testaments. In the Ten Commandments we read, "Thou shalt not commit adultery," and the Savior emphasized and amplified that injunction in His Sermon on the Mount when He said:

> Ye have heard that it was said by them of old time,
> Thou shalt not commit adultery:
> But I say unto you, That whosoever looketh on a woman to lust after her hath committed adultery with her already in his heart.
>
> —Matthew 5:27-28

Blessed are the pure in heart: for they shall see God.
—Matthew 5:8

The wisdom of this divine commandment is recognized by all civilized societies, even though it is often flagrantly disregarded. This commandment, like all of God's laws, is given for the benefit of His children. He had their welfare in mind, physical, social, and spiritual.

Birth into mortality is a necessary step in His divine plan. It involves the sacred, Godlike act of procreation which establishes eternal bonds with the continuing responsibility of home and family. A happy home life, solid and enduring family ties, associations, and disciplines, are all part of His plan to prepare people for eternal life. He declared it to be His work and glory to bring to pass the immortality and eternal life of man. — Moses 1:39.

This most intimate relationship between man and woman, authorized by God within the covenant of marriage, is not merely physical or biological. It involves the whole personality, affects the complex nature of men and women. This relationship, within the sanctity of the marriage covenant, with its concomitant obligations, makes man and woman one in interests, aims, aspirations, and responsibilities. If they are true to their covenants to each other, to their children, and to God, their whole beings are merged, they become one mentally and spiritually, and the family they establish is an eternal unit. Prerequisite to ideal marriage is deep and abiding love. This enduring relationship requires purity of thought, word, and action; devotion, loyalty, sacrifice, integrity, fidelity, honesty, and again unsullied virtue. There is no real decency without virtue, and there is no real happiness without decency.

The sin of unchastity, which in the Ten Commandments is listed among the "thou shalt nots," is often compounded of or calls in as allies most of the other misbehaviors known to man. The adversary intends it to be followed by a chain reaction on the sinner. He is never satisfied with one conquest but attempts to cut off all retreat by tempting his victim to follow detours into such downhill paths as lying, cheating, destroying the evidence of his guilt by killing the unborn victim of his lust. All this in reliance on the false promise of self-protection.

Lucifer and his agents have devised means by which men may partially protect themselves against the natural physical results of their indecency, and has thereby led many into sin by whispering the twin lies, "It is no longer dangerous," and "No one will ever know." With these false assurances, thousands, who might have been deterred by fear of consequences, have been lured into transgression.

Infidelity is the number one enemy of the home, which, like the termites, operates from the inside, destroying the underpinning and weakening the foundation.

A home of love cannot long endure if built upon the quicksands of lust. The cement in the foundation of the home is respect, including self-respect. When that cement is gone, both the character of the individuals and the home itself begins to disintegrate. Sin is always ugly and, especially in retrospect, it is repugnant.

Chastity throughout life, both before and during marriage, requires self-control, reverence for personality, respect for the rights of others, and for the laws of God. God's law of chastity is as binding on men as on women. Each has the same need and responsibility to be pure in heart.

The powerful sex drives are instinctive, which is to say, God-given, and therefore are not evil per se. In order that these instincts may be controlled and directed into proper channels, they should be indulged only within the divinely instituted sacrament of marriage. The home, under the divine plan, is intended to last throughout eternity. To protect its foundation is an obligation devolving upon both man and woman. There can be no double standard.

But one of the most lethal weapons used by Lucifer against the first offender is the disarming implication that, having once sinned there is no hope and that therefore he might just as well surrender and sample all of the other scented poisons prepared for his complete destruction.

Let all young pilgrims know that God is a Loving Father who stands ready to assist them. He understands the weaknesses of his children, and, if they fall and sincerely wish to rise again, they can rely upon His love and mercy and may obtain the blessings that follow true repentance. But let us all remember that in His economy there is an immutable penalty for every broken law.

In our own time the Lord has spoken unequivocally and repeatedly on this vital subject, and has underlined and emphasized His word as contained in the Ten Commandments, the Sermon on the Mount, and modern revelation.

In the Bible we read:

My son, keep thy father's commandment, and forsake not the law of thy mother:
Bind them continually upon thine heart, and tie them about thy neck. . . .
For the commandment is a lamp; and the law is light; . . .

To keep thee from the evil woman, from the flat-
tery of the tongue of a strange woman.

Lust not after her beauty in thine heart; neither
let her take thee with her eyelids.

Can a man take fire in his bosom, and his clothes
not be burned?

Can one go upon hot coals, and his feet not be
burned?

—Proverbs 6:20-21, 23-25, 27-28

III. Postrequisites

Maturing, a Continuing Process

YOU CAN KEEP YOUR MIND LIMBER BY STRETCHING IT OCCASIONALLY

The question, "When is a person mature?" is as difficult to answer as, "When is a person educated?" The answer in both cases is "Never." There are as many stages of maturity as there are of education. As the school of life continues throughout life, each of us should check up periodically on whether he is really maturing, growing, developing, or whether he has reached a point of arrested development, stopped growing, has arrived.

People cannot be classified and labeled on the basis of chronological age alone. Some people reach maturity much earlier than others. Maturing involves growing or developing physically, mentally, emotionally and spiritually. As one matures he becomes more capable of enjoying friends, family, work, leisure — life. We may determine the degree of one's development by noting his emotional reactions, whether they are adult or childish. With maturity should come dignity, resourcefulness, self control, a desire to give rather than to receive, the ability to compromise on minor issues, and see the other fellow's point of view.

A person should take pride in steadily maturing as it brings to him fulfillment of the promise of his budding years, a promise of completeness of growth and development. Steady maturing whets interest, adjusts perspective and balance, and brings values into focus. The word "mature"

does not connote a stationary status, being static or inactive. The mature adult is a maturing person who continues to enjoy the abundant life in all stages of his development. We must not deceive ourselves into thinking that lengthened years will automatically bring wisdom. Unless we keep some of the zest of youth, an interest in the things around us, and continue to hunger and thirst after knowledge, then old age may bring to us only a garrulous dotage. We are reminded in Ecclesiastes that

> Better is a poor and wise child than an old and foolish king, who will no more be admonished.
> —Ecclesiastes 4:13

And Job, in his tribulations, reminded Zophar that:

> With the ancient is widom; and in the length of days understanding.
> —Job 12:12

They who have no internal resources of happiness will be uneasy in every stage of life. Outward handicaps can be overcome by inward forces. There are, of course, physical limitations imposed by increasing years, but we should not yield or surrender to them, or give up in despair with the first twinge of stiffening joints in mind or body. Life will continue to have an alluring and increasing wealth of interest all the way down its western slopes for him who keeps a cutting edge on his awareness.

Being forced to give up certain kinds of work should not result in despair or loss of interest. There are many new experiences awaiting the prick of active curiosity at any age, but they will never come to us if we merely sit and think—or only sit.

While age may require us to lessen our demands on our heart and physical vigor, we should resist the temptation to submit weakly to psychological or imaginary limitations. If we would retain our resiliency of spirit as the years crowd upon us, we must with avidity seek new interests, new knowledge, and new experience. We must beware of the deterioration which is incipient in rigidity of mind.

There is an interesting chapter in the book of Ecclesiastes. I insert in parentheses some interpretations made by a Bible scholar, which may or may not be strictly accurate, but they make the passage vivid and applicable to older people in all lands.

> Remember now thy Creator in the days of thy youth, while the evil days come not, nor the years draw nigh, when thou shalt say, I have no pleasure in them;
>
> While the sun, or the light, or the moon, or the stars, be not darkened, nor the clouds return after the rain (failing eyesight):
>
> In the day when the keepers of the house (the hands) shall tremble, and the strong men (the legs) shall bow themselves, and the grinders (the teeth) cease because they are few, and those that look out of the windows (the eyes) be darkened,
>
> And the doors (the lips) shall be shut in the streets. When the sound of the grinding is low, and he shall rise up at the voice of the bird (inability to sleep), and all the daughters of musick shall be brought low (increasing deafness);
>
> Also when they shall be afraid of that which is high (shortness of breath), and fears shall be in the way (difficulty of walking), and the almond tree (grey hair) shall flourish, and the grasshopper

shall be a burden (inability to carry even a small weight), and desire (appetite and passion) shall fail; because man goeth to his long home, and the mourners go about the streets:

Or ever the silver cord be loosed, or the golden bowl be broken, or the pitcher be broken at the fountain, or the wheel broken at the cistern.
Then shall the dust return to the earth as it was: and the spirit shall return unto God who gave it.

                    —Ecclesiastes 12:1-7
                    These Harvest Years by
                    Janet H. Baird, pp. 282, 283,
                    Published by Doubleday

Ecclesiastes was written before the miracles of science made it possible to reduce the speed of diminishing vigor, extend man's life expectancy, restore man's eyesight, replace his teeth, amplify sound, and even tranquilize his sleep, but even with the aid of all these, man continues to grow old. What we are pleading for is that he will continue to mature as long as life shall last. And even after death the Lord has told us that "Whatsoever principal of intelligence we attain to in this life, it will rise with us in the resurrection, and if a person gains more knowledge and intelligence in this life through his diligence and obedience than another, he will have so much the advantage in the world to come."

Maturing, or growing old, and they are not always synonymous, should not be limited by definition to the rate of deterioration in the arteries, tissues and organs, which aging and the passing of time entails. One's maturity may be evaluated by noting his reaction to his surroundings, his interest in current events, the tempo of his thought and conversation.

The mature person confronts life with confidence. He thinks before he speaks, meditates and evaluates before he

acts. He foresees consequences and prepares to meet them. He knows that life has continuity and that in each period of life he may gain something which will be of value in the next. Planned, intelligent maturing has a sobering, mellowing, and polishing effect.

Some people continue to live a full and creative life through their eighties. The man who is enjoying a balanced maturity can avoid much of the stress and strain which tend to shorten life. Many of the physical disabilities of age can be avoided or tempered by obeying God's physical and spiritual laws. As we learn how to truly live, the challenge of the maturing years will be as exhilarating as were the years of youth.

If we can achieve serenity, and tranquility, and keep our zest, if we can attain peace within our hearts, and keep alive ambition, then each advancing year will bring its own reward and give us appetite for the next.

Maturing life can and should be rich and radiant at every period provided we really live and do not merely endure or tolerate our lot. Robert Browning put into the mouth of Rabbi Ben Ezra the following inspiring words:

> Therefore I summon age
> To grant youth's heritage . . .
>
> Youth ended, I shall try
> My gain or loss thereby:
> Leave the fire ashes, what survives is gold . . .
>
> My times be in Thy hand!
> Perfect the cup as planned!
> Let age approve of youth, and death complete
>   the same!

Satisfying maturity must have continuity, contact in both directions to guide and spur ambition: If youth and age will meet and mingle, work and play and plan together, both will profit by the contact. A bit of the dash and ven- turesome of youth will check the rust and errosion and natural wear of increasing age. The warmth and enthusiasm of youth can be carried into life's ocean like a gulf stream. Also age may minister to youth and, guided by the voice of experience, prevent disaster.

There are, of course, many things which affect for good or ill the maturing personality. The people with whom we work, the friends with whom we play, the neighbors with whom we visit, the authors of the books we read. The teach- ers and the students in our schools have a profound effect upon us as we move toward more maturity. Also the Church is a most important educational influence. It teaches us that faith in God will cast out fear, and fear is always a deterrent to emotional maturity. Fear and worry are the opposites of faith and trust.

There are some immature people in every community who regard themselves as fully mature. These are they who insist upon having their own way all the time, who bulldoze and bully their way through life and trample on the rights of others. When such people marry and get the authority of parenthood, the effect upon their children will be deplorable and ruinous. There you will find strong emo- tional stress and a family which, as an educational factor, is not only a failure but a menace.

Family counselors sometimes wish they could provide a sort of mental X-ray, a mirror for confused and unhappy people to examine their inmost souls. Such a self-appraising

look could give an accurate diagnosis of many of their ail-
ments, and a proper diagnosis often suggests a remedy.

Men and women, young and old, can make life exhilarating and zestful to the end by disciplining their mental and
emotional reactions. The person who loves life, who really
wants to live, who is too busy enjoying life to be bothered
with its pestiferous trivialities, can change the emotional
temperature of every life he touches, of every group he joins,
where all will be lifted up, encouraged, and blessed by the
touch of his inspiring personality.

Doctors tell us that more than 50% of all illnesses are
emotionally induced. In other words, most people are immature. Both physical symptoms and loss of equilibrium
can generally be traced to emotional upsets, unresolved antagonisms, doubts and apprehensions.

Marriage counselors, lawyers, and church leaders often
meet couples who seek the services of the court or church
and wish to formalize and finalize what has already
taken place between them. They are no longer married but
only undivorced. They are unhappy children who unwisely
tackled an adult problem, or in the maturing process have
grown along divergent lines.

And then sometimes the interview is with a broken-
hearted wife, whose husband has "left her behind" because
she failed to "keep up with him." As the interview continues
it becomes apparent that the reason she could not keep up
with him intellectually was because she worked long hours
outside the home to make it possible for him to complete
his education, and "after working hours" she kept up the
house, cooked the meals, cared for the children, and inci-

dentally, wore the same dress and coat for three years, all to the end that he might get "his chance."

In other words, she made him what he is and then he has the impudence, effrontery, and audacity to feel superior to her and to go off with some girl who has spent all her time and thought upon herself. Such a man is more despi-cable than a drunkard or a wife beater or a lazy lout who won't provide for his children. He is truly beneath contempt and his new self-centered wife will probably prove it to him.

On the other hand, sometimes the wife outstrips her husband by selfishly keeping up with the times and the neigh-bors, while the husband is saddled with his daily tasks dur-ing the day and then often does the housework after he gets home at night.

Tell Him (Her) So

How do I love thee. Let me count the ways.
I love thee to the depth and breadth and height
My soul can reach, when feeling out of sight
For the ends of Being and ideal Grace. . . .
I love thee with a love I seemed to lose
With my lost saints,—I love thee with the breath,
Smiles, tears, of all my life! and, if God choose
I shall but love thee better after death.

—Elizabeth Barrett Browning

Despite trials, tempests, and tensions in the rough and tumble of everyday living, the matrimonial ship can be so constructed and kept in repair as to make it seaworthy whatever the weather. The moving tides beneath the surface, "too deep for sound or foam," where true love anchors, need not be affected by the ripples or even the high waves on the surface of the ocean.

When the husband and wife tell each other of their affection and demonstrate it by their conduct by both what they do and refrain from doing, then their marriage, like the tides of the ocean, will not be seriously disturbed by surface storms. Love is a wonderful ballast.

While deep feelings of affection are too sacred for flaunting, each person in love, especially after marriage, should seek every opportunity to display affections in the home. Love is the key that unlocks the inner feeling of the heart, and it must not be lost or allowed to rust through

disuse. Any key that rests will rust. Serenity, peace, and poise are found in the truly loving heart that has found response in another heart. To all who seek and trust Him the Master's words, "Peace be still" will be as effective during the storms of life as they were on the Sea of Galile.

The best example we know of happy and successful married life is the inspiring example of President and Sister David O. McKay, loved and revered by all members of the Church, and by thousands of others. For fifty-nine years they have lived what he has so consistently advocated in almost every country of the world, and epitomized in a recent article from which we quote.

> I sincerely believe that too many couples come to the marriage altar looking upon the ceremony as the end of courtship.
>
> Let all the members of the Church look upon that ceremony as the beginning of an eternal courtship. Let us not forget that during the burdens of home life tender words of appreciation and courteous acts are even more appreciated than during those sweet days and months of courtship.
>
> It is after the ceremony, and during the trials that daily arise in the home that a word of "thank you, pardon me, if you please," contributes to the perpetuation of that love which brought you to the altar.
>
> Keep in mind three great ideals that contribute to happiness after the marriage ceremony.
>
> First, LOYALTY. You have no right, young man, to yield to the attention of any young woman other than that sweet wife, and you, husband, have no right even to attract the attention of

another man's wife. Her duty is with her husband, building a home. Loyalty to the great convenant made at that altar!

Second, SELF-CONTROL. Little things annoy, and you speak quickly, sharply, loudly, and wound the other's heart. I know of no virtue that helps to contribute to the happiness and peace of a home more than the great quality of self-control in speech. Refrain from saying the sharp word that comes to your mind at once if you are wounded or if you see something in the other that offends you. In a few minutes you will be glad that you did not say the harsh word, that you did not commit the impulsive act, and the result is love and peace in the home.

The third ideal is that little simple virtue of COURTESY—parents courteous to their children, and children courteous to father and mother, and there is an element of refinement in the home, LOYALTY, SELF-CONTROL, COURTESY.

Fifteen years, thirty years, fifty years, and throughout eternity—be just as courteous to each other as you were when you courted. It makes a happy home. I know of no other place where happiness abides more surely than in the home. It is possible to make home a bit of heaven. Indeed, I picture heaven as a continuation of the ideal home.

In the marriage relationship, if love is to be kept alive and growing, it must be expressed in kindly words and thoughtful actions. Where either party takes for granted that the other knows he is loved and never tells him of it, much of the color and beauty of life will fade and what should be zestful, joy-giving companionship degenerates into

lackluster, humdrum existence. The marriage will not go on the rocks if each lover continues to feel the security and warmth of hearing repeatedly, "I love you."

Couples should realize that if their marriage is to succeed they must, with eternal vigilance, keep their love growing by nourishing and cultivating it constantly.

Daily investments in mutual compliments pay wonderful dividends in family solidarity, understanding, and success. There is no woman but who likes to have her husband tell her he loves her, wishes to be with her, how to him she is the best-dressed woman in town, how he likes her hairdo and even her kitchen apron. Complimenting her on her appearance, her cooking, and housekeeping will prove to be a wonderful tonic to her sometimes wilting spirit. Weary men too may be revived by a word of praise, confidence, and love. "I married the best man in the world" is music to any husband's soul — and it may sweeten his tongue and soothe a temper, worn thin in the day's grind.

Little acts of tenderness, kindness, and consideration continued through life, will make the tree of love everbearing, like orange trees, with buds, blossoms, and ripened fruit the year round. Love in December can and should be as warm as it was in June — and even sweeter.

The small courtesies sweeten life; the greater ennoble it.—Bovee

It is not only what we do that tends to break up our marriages, but what we fail to do. There is an old proverb which says, "What he was saying to her was drowned out by what he did not do." The husband lying on the couch in the front room, may shout to his wife in the

kitchen and say, "Honey, I love you," but it would be much more convincing if he would express it by taking a dish towel or a broom to help a bit. Sometimes a man says to his wife, "I love you," but his conduct says more loudly, "I love me."

If the light of love has been kept aglow by tenderness, thoughtfulness, kindness, and understanding, if a touch of the hand, the sound of a footstep on the stairs, continues through the years to bring a romantic thrill or quickening of the heart beat, then the zest of April and of June will not diminish in December. People who are capable of dis' interested affection attest that pure love is the greatest thing in the world. Jesus said:

> A new commandment I give unto you, That ye love one another; as I have loved you, that ye also love one another — John 13:34

Someone has said that all the water in the world cannot sink a ship unless it gets inside the ship, and that all the trouble in the world cannot sink a man unless it gets inside his mind. So it is with marriage. If its stresses and strains and difficulties are courageously met and co-operatively dealt with in an adult manner, without recriminations, charges, and countercharges, if, in other words, these inevitable diffi' culties can be kept objective or peripheral, they will not get into the hearts of the persons concerned, and the matrimonial ship can be kept afloat, whatever the weather.

Both husband and wife should keep a sense of humor. They should laugh with each other. Lincoln is reported to have said on one occasion, "If I could not hear or tell a good story occasionally, I would die; humor is the oxygen of my soul." Does your homecoming mean the rising or the setting

of the sun to wife and children? Must they get a "weather report" on your moods before submitting a personal budget or suggesting a family holiday? How often do you laugh and play with them? A poignant story is told of a little boy who ran to his mother, and clutching at her apron said, "Mama, I saw Daddy laughing on the street corner with some other men. I didn't know he could laugh."

Each needs the assurance and reassurance of the other's love and laughter. The love that is not nurtured by repeated endearments and refreshed by a bit of humor is liable to wither and die on the vine. "I like not only to be loved but to be told that I am loved. The realm of silence is large enough beyond the grave."

They do not love that do not show their love.

—Shakespeare

Loving and being loved bring peace of soul and tranquility. Love answers love; it, like a boomerang, comes back to him who sends it out. Thus one who truly loves not only experiences peace of soul, but, what is even more blessed he has the joy of bringing peace to others' souls.

Upon being asked by a distraught husband what he could do to prove to his wife that he loved her and to get her to call off the divorce, the writer suggests the following:

1.   Give her a regular monthly allowance.

2.   Take her some flowers or some small unexpected present occasionally.

3.   Tell her every day that you love her and then prove it.

4.   When she asks for $10.00 (she shouldn't need to ask), give her $20.00.

5.   Tell her of your business problems and take her advice once in a while.

6.   Say, "Let's go to a show tonight. I've arranged for a baby sitter."

Love cannot endure solitary confinement. Its life-giving sunbeams, when wafted into all life's activities, will dispel gloom as light dispels darkness.

Conjugal affection should not be kept in tightly corked bottles. It must be poured before it can be tasted. Love's perfume must be diffused by the atomizer of repeated declaration if its aroma is to sweeten the atmosphere of daily living.

Blessed is the family where love is diffused and absorbed atmospherically where it is avowed not alone by endearing words, but by facial expressions, little thoughtful acts of kindness, unexpected gifts which are not dictated by the calendar. "There is beauty all around" in such a home, and all who come within its radiance are lifted up and blessed.

Yes, let us tell them that we love them, and not assume they know it. I think it was a Scotsman who said, at his wife's bier, "She was a good and lovely lady and once I almost told her so." Sometimes silence is cruel.

> The clever folks can give us knowledge of the highest worth—the secrets of philosophy, the wonders of the earth; the science of the universe— yet this one truth I've found: It's Love that is the greatest thing—and makes the world go round.

A little word; a simple word; and yet it means so much; Love is the strongest force, and underneath its magic touch—a heart unfolds just like a flower that opens to the sun. . . . This is the sweetest thing in life—when all is said and done.

—Patience Strong
From *The Sunny Side*

Enriching Life Together

Are we not one? Are we not join'd by heaven?
Each interwoven with the other's fate?
Are we not mix'd like streams of meeting rivers,
Whose blended waters are no more distinguish'd,
But roll into the sea one common flood.

—Rowe

Too often the joy of being together fades or becomes insipid unless both husband and wife are on the alert, seeking to develop new facets of interest, new luster, each trying to make the other happy and to keep zest, humor, verve, and imagination in their partnership.

In a recent article in the *Reader's Digest,* January, 1959, some pertinent suggestions were given for making marriage happier and more exciting. By permission we quote the following:

What a Husband Can Do:
Bring her flowers while she can still smell them.
Even if you've been married a long time, compliment her cooking.
Ask your wife's advice on business problems and sometimes take it.
Learn some new jokes for the sake of your wife, who has heard the old ones so often.
Send presents to your wife for no reason at all.

What a Wife Can Do:

Don't make him the family "meany." Don't say to the children, "Just wait until your father gets home" or "I want to let you, but Daddy says no."

Don't tell him your problems until you've fed him. , Remember the things you said and did to land him and try them again.

Don't shush your husband if he sings at parties or acts the clown.

Be home when he gets there.

Don't borrow his razor.

Don't give him surprise parties.

What You Both Can Do:

Treat each other occasionally as though you were meeting for the first time.

Never sleep on a problem without a solution or some agreement.

Have a big family Bible; read together from it and enter family records in it.

Stop keeping up with the Joneses.

Avoid getting mad at the same time.

Respect each other's privacy.

Don't sacrifice all your fun today for what you think may be security tomorrow.

Switch off the TV and talk.

Build each other up in public. Don't try to compete.

Now that you have finished reading this article, tell your spouse that you are glad you married him or her and that you would do it all over again.

The routine of daily home life is liable to become dull and monotonous and the joy of togetherness lose zest unless both parties find or make some variety or novelty and especially cultivate good humor.

There is great satisfaction in giving and receiving little thoughtful attentions, little boosts to the ego. There is a core of childishness in most men which responds to trivial attentions.

In most happy and smooth running marriages we find a wife who tries to please her husband in a dozen small ways each day. She's a diplomat who is likely to get a favorable agreement on major matters. She wins her way into almost every area of living. She keeps the delicate machinery of family life well oiled and running smoothly by little drops of thoughtfulness expertly applied where there's friction. Let us practice patience, tolerance, forgiveness, forbearance and the divine willingness to forget private wants and peeves. Recriminations and self-pity lead to the psychiatrist's couch or the divorce court.

Blessed is the couple who both enjoy good health, but even if one or both are handicapped they may still live abundantly. Too many parents, especially the mothers, while children are coming into the home, neglect or impair their health and thereby do a disservice to the family. Young married couples and those of middle age, as well as the aged, should have regular medical checkups. There should be no gap between pediatrics and geriatrics. There are first-class physicians in almost every community, and provision should be made in the annual budget for their valuable services. Prevention is not only better but also less expensive than cure.

From the department of vital statistics, we learn that at the time of the American Revolution the average life span in this country was 35.5 years. By 1900 it had risen to 50 years, and today it is 65 years for men and 71 for

women. But what we are concerned with in this chapter is that, in the words of the Gerontological Society, we "add life to years, not only years to life." We are not here concerned merely with prolonging our stay on this planet, although most of us wish to live as long as possible, but let us continue to cram our years full of life, as we hope and work for joyous old age.

Without discussing the medical factors involved, there are many things that we can do to prolong our lives. Oliver Wendell Holmes once said, "If you are setting out to achieve three score years and twenty, the first thing to be done is, some years before birth, advertise for a couple of parents, both belonging to long-lived families." We shall not here discuss the relative merits of the arguments of the past on heredity vs. environment, but we do call attention to the fact that almost any young couple, by working together, can enrich and extend their lives and thereby achieve the purpose of life — the attainment of joy. As one who did not mind mixing metaphors said, "A stitch in time is worth a pound of cure."

The young couple who are seeking to enrich their lives together should, in the interest of health and happiness, acquire the habit of moderation in all things, and abstain entirely from some things which are not good for man. Use of liquor in the home destroys the admiration and respect upon which successful marriages are based. All should be warned against becoming morbid about sickness or disease, even though they may think they have inherited certain tendencies. Doctors tell us it is just as harmful to be over-solicitous about one's health as it is to be careless about it. The value of these enriching years together depends in large

measure upon mind and heart, upon new interest and new knowledge, for when one stops learning, he stops living. Inasmuch as the couple are to live together, they should learn together, and thereby grow together. There should be more equality in the marriage.

> Not from his head was woman took,
> As made her husband to o'erlook;
> Not from his feet, as one designed
> The footstool of the stronger kind;
> But fashioned for himself, a bride;
> An equal, taken from his side.
> —Charles Leslie

Preserving and developing a sense of humor, optimism, and vision will enrich these middle adult years. Men should not lose their buoyancy, nor women their charm, and both should resist the tendency to become sensitive, critical, possessive, or domineering.

This program of enjoying things together, which begins in courtship, should not lapse, but continue through the early, middle, and later married years. The couple should not wait until the days of their active parenthood is past before undertaking their joint project of enriching life. If they have not learned along the way to be delightful, lively, interesting, and inquisitive, then when their active parenthood days are past, there is danger of their seeking the chimney corner, where, as querulous old people, they may huddle and commiserate.

> Love reckons hours for months, and days for years;
> And every little absence is an age.
> —Dryden, "Amphytrion"

That man is not wise who spends all his energies making money, nor the woman whose spare time is spent playing cards or visiting at the club. If these middle years are to be enriched, and if the couple are to enjoy them together, there must be mutuality of interest, of outlook, and of activity. One of the saddest situations this author met while counseling was a wealthy thirty-six year old man who could no longer eat, sleep, or concentrate on anything, on the edge, as he said, of a complete nervous breakdown. He was accompanied by an attractive woman, also in her thirties, for whom life had lost all interest, and even her card parties, her clubs, and her dinners could not distract her mind or divert it from pursuing its orbit around her self-centered monotony.

Each young couple should, from the start, practice economy and frugality, but they should not allow money-making to become the center of their lives. So many things turn to ashes when we get them. Many men spend their life-time seeking things they spurn when they have found them, and meanwhile their wives have sought diversion and fought boredom and discouragement.

Pressure of business is a poor alibi for failing to diversify one's interests or to join the spouse in search of the happiness which money cannot buy.

Certainly the family's comfort and security must be given priority, but to comfort and security there should be added warmth and community of interest. Mutual interest and planned activity together, while the couple are still in the active years of parenthood, will pay big dividends when the richly rewarding harvest time of later years is reached. They who increase their mutual awareness as they come along the

way will thereby increase their aliveness and have no time or desire to think of retirement or idleness. To most people, voluntary retirement proves to be a sad illusion, a one-way street with a tombstone at the end. People should continue through the years to be busy, to be occupied, to be useful and needed, to be serviceable to others and inspiring to youth. As these later years come on they will be able to fill their lives with the things they have always wanted to do.

Let us stay in the game and play in the game, though changing years may indicate the need for changing positions on the team. Unless one is mentally or physically handi-capped, he should never voluntarily go to the benches in the bull pen.

Dr. Maxwell Gittleson, as quoted in *These Harvest Years* by Janet H. Baird, and published by Doubleday, set up some guideposts to sound mental health in later years. He says it is important:

1. Never to know that one is through.
2. Never to feel superfluous.
3. Never to lack significance.
4. Never to be without use.
5. Never to be without an outlet for the creative urge.
6. Never to be without a word in the affairs of men.

No period of our lives is all sweetness. If it were it would be nauseating. Each has its dilemmas, its difficulties, and its lessons. But these mature years together should and can be among the richest. At this time of life we should have learned something about our capacities and our limitations and realize that what happens to us is not as important as what we do with what happens to us.

All growth involves change and change requires adjust-ment. We should seek to retain not only our versatility, but our elasticity. All life is growth—menaced constantly by deterioration—its purpose is more life, more joy.

This period of enriching years is but a continuation of the years that went before and should be enriched and hallowed by the memory of what has been. Looking back we realize that each day thus far has had its own heart-breaks and misgivings, but also its successes and its triumphs. As we think of the happiness of our own childhood, we re-member that we sometimes resented the discipline and re-straint, but now, as the lens of time begins to bring things into focus and perspective, we see how discipline and re-straint contributed to our happiness and made it lasting.

Sometimes we are a bit nostalgic about our adolescent years when we wanted the world to get out of our way, when we wanted to say and do what had never been said or done before, but now we see that the interference of our elders almost kept us from making fools of ourselves and this memory adds to life's pattern a thread of humor.

And then we think of the early struggles for education and preparation for life, leading into the deeper problems of young married life and parenthood. Assuredly they were trying years, and sometimes they almost pried us apart, but now, in middle life, when our children are marrying off, and we see them starting the cycle all over again, we clasp hands and admit that most of what happened to us was for our good, and that a wise and loving Father had his hand upon our shoulders.

Those of us who know the pathos of the leaf when
"sere and yellow,"
We, who in life's garden, feel that frost is in the
air,
Often think of early springtime and look back instead of forward,
As the coming of life's winter brings its whiteness
to our hair.

There's no turning back to harbor once we've
launched upon the voyage;
We must sail with dauntless courage and with faith
to chart the way.
We'll be judged, not by the speed with which we
travel,
But by the cargo we've collected from the ports
along the way.

from *Eternal Quest*

The Spirit of the Home

Except the Lord build the house, they labour in
vain that build it. . . .
—Psalm 127:1

There are as many pleasant things, as many
 pleasant tones
For those who dwell by cottage hearths as those
 who sit on thrones.
—Phoebe Cary

The builders of homes—houses and furnishings are
incidental—make a more valuable contribution to the present
and the future than the builders of great fortunes, the authors
of great books, or the legislators who put our laws on the
statute books.

The real homebuilder does not spend all his energies
in pursuit of wealth, honor or fame, which, when compared
with the happy homes, are but "vanity and vexation of
spirit." In the happy home we have complete understanding
and intellectual sympathy between and among its founders
and its occupants. Heaven itself is but an extension of a
happy home. In fact, we have a trinity here, though not yet
quite divine, but every real home must have man, woman,
and child.

President McKay has written:

  The second essential, fundamental element in
the building and in the perpetuity of a great people
is the home. "The strength of a nation, especially
of a republican nation, is in the intelligent and
well-ordered homes of the people." If and when

the time comes that parents shift to others or to the state the responsibility of rearing their children, the stability of the nation will be undermined and its impairment and disintegration will have begun.

I praise God for the instructions He has given His people regarding the sacredness, the sanctity, and permanence of the family relationship.

Let us teach youth that the marriage relation is one of the most sacred obligations known to man, or that man can make. Teach them that the family is the first institution ordained of God, and instituted among men. If every couple sensed the sacredness of this obligation, there would be fewer homes broken up by disagreements that lead to divorces. The safety, the perpetuity of our government, or of any republican form of government, depend upon the safety and permanency of the home. Herein we get a glimpse of one thing in which this people may be the saviors, in a way, of this great nation. The home is the place where the perpetuation of the principles of liberty as well as the instructions in the gospel of Jesus Christ should be given to the children. When the home breaks up, then the children begin to wander off into sin. Then the law must reach out to bring them back and try to teach them some principles of service, and principles of true government; but oh, how helpless, how helpless the state, when the home has failed!

Homes are made permanent through love. If you feel that you have not the love of those little boys and girls, study to get it. Though you neglect some of the cattle, though you fail to produce good crops, even, study to hold your children's love.

—*Pathways to Happiness,*
pp. 3, 113

Morning prayer together conditions the family for the day's problems and in the evening, prayer is the balm which relieves tensions, soothes weariness, and encourages peaceful slumber. For the father to pray before the children and thank God for his wife, for her virtues, her sacrifice, her service, is to implant in their hearts a lasting impression that their mother is really something special; and let the mother pray for the father and thank God for him and for his virtues, even though some of them may be in anticipation. When the children hear such prayers, both parents gain stature and respect in the minds of the children. Prayer brings the "Peace be still" to the sometimes troubled waters of married life.

No man can be successful in the larger sense who has never married, and no failure is more complete than failure to measure up to the standard set by the Master Himself for the head of the house:

> For the husband is the head of the wife, even as Christ is the head of the Church: . . .
> Husbands, love your wives, even as Christ . . . loved the church, and gave himself for it;
>
> —Ephesians 5:23, 25

T. DeWitt Talmage wrote:

> Home! It is a charmed word! Through that one syllable thrills untold melody, and the laughter of children; the sound of well-known footsteps and the voices of undying affection. Home! I hear in that word the ripple of meadow brooks, in which knee-deep we waded, the lowing of cattle coming up from the pasture, the sharp hiss of the scythe amid the thick grass, the breaking of the hay-rick where we trampled down the load.

Home! Upon that word there drops the sunshine of beauty and the shadow of tender sorrows, the reflection of ten thousand voices and fond memories.

There are very few songs which are as universally known, or which touch the heart strings quite as tenderly as "Home Sweet Home." Most of us remember best the songs our mothers used to sing because the memory of them retains the atmosphere of home. There are few sweeter things in life than the almost haunting memories of childhood days and thoughts of home and family.

Wherever we may travel, and however interesting the voyage or the countries we may visit, whether it be the history-laden lands of Europe, or the enchanting isles of the South Pacific, if all lands and climes were rolled into one they could not equal in sweetness, the charm or value the homes of our childhood or the homes which we ourselves are building. When one comes to his own doorstep, after traveling far and wide, a rich contentment falls upon him and like a monarch he enters his kingdom — his castle— his home.

We admonish young married couples to make their homes the center of their interests. They may reach out into business or professional life, or seek careers, or travel much, but let them keep their moorings in the home. The person who marries for love builds a home, and then keeps love alive, is the richest and happiest person in the world.

Another insurance against divorce is religious conviction and activity on the part of husband and wife. The refining influence of religion in the home and in public worship is indispensable to enduring happiness. Statistics show

there are fewer divorces in the truly religious homes. In one survey made by judges of district courts, it was found that in the years since 1933 only two couples have come to the legal aid society seeking divorce where both husband and wife were active in Church work and living up to the standards of the Church. The spirit of dissension, strife, bickering, quarreling, recrimination, and fault-finding is incompatible with the spirit of the gospel. Religion, like light, dispels darkness and fear.

Some of our best homes are among the middle income class. Our greatest men have come from good homes. It is here that boys are taught honor, thrift, industry, and independence. It is here that daughters are taught the true meaning of love, how to make and keep a home, and are prepared for the responsibilities of wifehood and the hallowed role of motherhood.

The man who wins the love of a good girl, and with her establishes a home, has great wealth and riches, though it be a humble cottage

> "Marriage hath more of safety than the single life," says Jeremy Taylor; "it hath not more ease, but less danger; it is more merry and more sad; it is fuller of sorrows, and fuller of joys; it lies under more burdens, but is supported by all the strength of love and charity, and those burdens are delightful. Marriage is the mother of the world, and preserves kingdoms, fills cities and churches, and peoples heaven itself."

No allurements of money, place, or power should be allowed to interfere with the primary purpose of life, the building of a home, the rearing of a family.

How unfortunate it is that so many of us put on our worst behavior in the home. It should be the happiest, sweet-est, most cheerful place on earth. It is a retreat for the har-assed and tired man, a haven for the wanderer, a holy citadel, protected and defended by a true and loving wife while her husband is away, and a place of comfort and seclusion, where he can lave his weary nerves and spirit in the warmth of her affection.

Happy is the couple whose love endures and is increased and multiplied with the arrival of the children. To them their home is Eden and love can keep the tempter out.

> Beloved, let us love one another: for love is of God; and every one that loveth is born of God; and knoweth God.
>
> He that loveth not knoweth not God; for God is love.
>
> In this was manifested the love of God toward us, because that God sent his only begotten Son into the world, that we might live through him.
>
> Herein is love, not that we loved God, but that he loved us, and sent his Son to be the propitiation for our sins.
>
> Beloved, if God so loved us, we ought also to love one another.
>
> —I John 4:7-11

Home is the residence of the heart as well as a place to feed and rest the body. If love and affection are not there, it becomes merely a house. It should be the object and am-bition of all young married couples to establish and maintain a home of love and laughter, where happy children may be unafraid, and where young people love to come. There is

no finer scene in all our country than a happy fireside. "The hearthstone is the cornerstone of civilization."

A house is built of logs and stone,
Of tiles and posts and piers;
A home is built of loving deeds
That stand a thousand years.
—Victor Hugo

Young people should realize that getting married is a continuing process, and that a happy home is the best place for that process to be carried out. Continuing to strengthen the bonds which hold the home together insures a fulfillment of the purpose of the home, and that really happens only when the two who preside therein are really and truly in love, for "Love is the fulfillment of the law."

Next in importance to love in the home is service, freely and joyfully rendered. Little acts of kindness, gentleness, and thoughtfulness are the distinguishing characteristics of a happy home.

The story is told of a fond wife in England, who was married to a general. She had driven to meet him at a railway station and told the footman to go and find the general. The servant, who was a new one and had been engaged in his master's absence, asked, "But how shall I know him?" "Oh," replied the lady, "look for a tall gentlemen helping somebody." The description was sufficient. The servant went and found the general helping an old lady out of a railroad carriage.

Most happily married men, if they were asked the secret of their success, their happiness, and usefulness, would doubt' less reply, "My wife, the queen of my home, the mother of my children."

As we visit the great art galleries of the world we are impressed by the discovery that their most enduring fame rests upon the simplest of their painted subjects — country scenes and cottages, firesides and families, and best of all, the Madonna or the Madonna and child.

Don't be bound and fettered by the shackles of routine—Home should have a character — it isn't a machine . . . It's the folks who live in it on whom you should expend your thought and care— It's human things that matter in the end.

Home is not the mere material things that we possess—Home is meant for comfort and domestic happiness . . . Home should harbour peace and love and rich tranquility — Visible and outward sign of inward harmony.

—Patience Strong
The Sunny Side

IV. The Family

Parenthood

O woman! lovely woman! Nature made thee
To temper man; we had been brutes without you;
Angels are painted fair, to look like you:
There's in you all that we believe of Heaven,
Amazing brightness purity, and truth,
Eternal joy, and everlasting love.
                    —Thomas Otway, "Venice Preserved"

The spirit, atmosphere, and environment of the home give significance and value to the house and its furnishings. Whether it be a cottage or a castle, moderately or extravagantly furnished, the home that is filled with loyalty, love, and laughter, where there are mutual confidence, understanding, and affection, where the home is sanctified by daily prayer and purified by the presence of a saintly mother, and a righteous father, there is a home built upon the rock; it will withstand the rains, the floods, and all of the vicissitudes of life.

The old-fashioned home—and there are still many of them—was not only the mother's habitat, it was her profession, where the bearing, nursing, and rearing of children was her dedicated task. Included in her God-given assignment was the hardly less important daily duty of maintaining in the home a spirit and environment conductive to physical, mental, and spiritual development. There was a quiet and unostentatious culture in these early homes and from them came some of our greatest citizens.

Dr. John A. Widtsoe said: "Love begets love. Whenever Latter-day Saints live and love together, their armor and their shield and all their weapons are of heavenly workmanship. The forces of evil flee in terror before them. Try it; the results never fail. The heart beats so warmly under the power of unselfish love. Whoever allows himself to cause contention or to spread it, whatever the means employed, plays into the hands of the devil and helps him win victory out of his sullen corner of defeat.

"Who would be the devil's tool?"

Today many people rush into the divorce courts with no other grounds to allege than incompatibility and that usually means they are living in an atmosphere of strained relations, high tensions, and smouldering resentments, with a quick temper as a fuse and a sharp tongue as an igniting spark.

In order to predetermine what spirit is to abide in and permeate the home they who are to build and occupy it should agree, before marriage, on the purpose of their joint project and the goal toward which they are to strive. There will, of course, be intermediate goals along the way, but these must be constantly used as steppingstones.

The couple should be concerned if they find they are pursuing their goals along parallel lines. Marriage involves a meeting and a merging until there is physical, mental, and spiritual oneness. To merge is to grow together, to unite, combine or coalesce without losing identity, self-confidence, or self-respect. Successful marriage involves sacrifice, selfless service, and co-operative effort.

Life is an unfolding process requiring many adjustments to changing conditions, but married life requires the couple to travel to the end of the road together. They must be mutually helpful in this joint unfolding and maturing process. It requires patience and perseverence to bring any bud to full bloom, whether it be a plant or a person. It requires infinite patience to await nature's creative processes. We must not "tear the close-shut leaves apart" but instead we must provide a suitable climate for continued growth toward colorful blossoms and rich fruit. Neither spouse should be guilty of blighting the other's natural development by the withering winds of harping criticism. Some of us have witnessed the melancholy spectacle of incessant belittling, a planned campaign of confidence-killing resulting in a hopeless complex of inferiority.

Sometimes when one feels inferior to his mate and is unable or unwilling to narrow the gap which separates them by raising himself, he attempts to even things up by pulling the other down to his own level. He does this by magnifying little faults, subjecting his mate to indignities and embarrassment before friends or strangers, forgetting for the moment the fact that his spouse is part of himself and that his destructive conduct is therefore suicidal.

It is vicious to destroy self-confidence deliberately and discourage attempts at self-improvement by embarrassing criticisms or denunciations of either the mate or the children. He who attempts to inflate his own ego by deflating another sins against both, and the penalty is certain. Inflation is not solid growth. Swelling is not development. Love is not puffed up.

So ought men to love their wives as their own
bodies. He that loveth his wife loveth himself.

—Ephesians 5:28

The spirit of the home created and maintained by the
parents determines the quality of its product. Economists
point to the home as the nursery of thrift, industry, and prosperity of the nation. Doctors, philosophers, and church
leaders assure us that the health, happiness, intelligence,
and character of our people depend upon the home. It is
subordinate to nothing else in our society. The spirit of
the homes in which we were raised and which we ourselves establish should condition us for exaltation in the
life to come. The home is essentially a religious institution, and the parents are charged with the responsibility
not only of building its foundations in religious ceremony
and moral conduct, but also of making sure that the spirit of
the gospel pervades every part thereof, for in the last analy-
sis the products of the home are spiritual.

Our Heavenly Father, the divine founder of the home—
He Himself established the first family—trusts His children
to maintain its integrity, its purity and high purpose; this
continuing trust repels the insidious appeals of selfishness,
vanity, and infidelty

They who enter into the eternal covenant of marriage
assume the sacred responsibility of guiding, instructing, and
training their children that they may qualify as beneficiaries
under this eternal bond, the sanctity and sanction of which
extend beyond the grave. We should all be reminded, however, that though this bond is intended to be eternal, the
corroding effects of sin may deprive all concerned of its
promised blessings.

If we hope to maintain the religious principles upon which our nation was founded, principles which are the hope of the world we must teach and practice them in our homes. We wish that with every flag unfurled there could be a scroll bearing the words, "God bless our home." The loftiest destiny of man and woman can be achieved in and through the happy home. It is the seedbed of the greatest beauty in this world and the next.

When the days become monotonously similar and the routine boring, someone must have the wit, or genius, to inject a challenging thought, a diverting activity, a bit of humor, or to call attention to the inspiring goal toward which the family journeys; someone must sing a song or raise a torch.

> "Though the way was steep and long
> And through a dark and lonely land,
> God placed upon my lips a song
> And put a lantern in my hand."

Self-Discipline and Self-Fulfilment

> Oh, it is great, and there is no other greatness,—
> to make one nook of God's creation more fruitful,
> better, more worthy of God; to make some human
> heart a little wiser, manlier, happier, — more
> blessed, less accursed.—
>   —Carlyle

"Men are, that they might have joy," said the prophet. We all yearn for lasting happiness, but there is no lasting happiness without self-respect. Therefore, we make self-fulfilment dependent upon self-discipline in our caption. This conjunction is most pertinent in marriage as there the self is a complex welding of male and female. Marriage affords life's greatest opportunity for self-fulfilment. It requires constant discipline to give and take graciously in the process of growing into the larger self.

Our capacity for enjoyment enlarges as we develop and discipline our mental, moral, physical, and temperamental equipment. We use the word *equipment* purposely as happiness or a capacity for happiness is born in us. The seeds of happiness were planted in us; it was not and will not be showered full-grown upon us. Therefore, a capacity for happiness is part of life's equipment. As we develop this capacity, we achieve a balanced, integrated personality. The search for joy is an eternal quest, and the married couple must seek it hand in hand, for neither man nor woman can achieve the highest degree of joy without a companion. There is really no such thing as eternal single blessedness.

The young married couple must not only grow together, but must make sure they are *growing* together. They should develop what has been called "a divine discontent." While it is a virtue to make do with what one has, it is a greater virtue to make the most of what one has, both of things and of personality.

Complacency and contentment are not synonymous. One finds real contentment when one has achieved a purpose, but having achieved it, one must not allow it to lose its value through complacency. That which we look forward to as intermediate goals must become launching pads and not burial grounds for enterprise and ambition.

Real success is never static. It is always fluid; is something ever more about to be. We must learn to apply the lessons of yesterday as we do the work of today, plan for tomorrow's activity, and face it unafraid.

It takes self-discipline to select a good book rather than a western on the TV, to enjoy a home evening with the family rather than go to a second-rate movie, to keep the mind in gear rather than let it idle, to think worth-while thoughts in moments of relaxation, to read and memorize a verse while waiting for an appointment or a meal.

When one gets a vision of himself as he wants to be, and as he knows he is capable of becoming, he must start on the endless job of self-fulfilment. The rate of self-improvement may be accelerated by persistent self-discipline.

Each person should stand himself up against the wall occasionally and look himself over, be honest in his self-appraisal, and if he is not satisfied with what he sees, he should have the courage and the good sense to do something about it.

You may be what you will be.
  Let cowards find their false content
In that poor word, environment;
  But spirit scorns it and is free.

It conquers time, it masters space,
  It cows the boastful trickster, chance,
And bids the tyrant circumstance
  Uncrown and fill a servant's place.

The human will, that force unseen,
  The offspring of a deathless soul
Can hew its way to any goal
  Though walls of granite intervene.

                                   —Author Unknown

It is well to check up occasionally on progress made toward self-improvement and self-fulfilment. Changing times
and the change in us require constant adjustments. Growth
and self-realization involve overcoming bad habits of thought,
speech, and conduct by substituting good ones. When we
have, by self-analysis, discovered just what kind of persons
we are, we should compare the truth with what we try
to make people think we are. Compare what people think
they see in us with what we really see in ourselves. Overcome deceit and make-believe, improve our personalities
and our characters, and know day by day that we can be
what we want to be if we want it persistently. We must
compare our actualities with our potentialities, break through
our chrysalis, and fly out on the variegated wings of ambition.

Men are sometimes referred to as animals, and some
men call other men insects. Call us what you will, we must
get beyond the larvae or the pupa stage of development,
if we are to know the joy of spreading our wings to the
lifting winds of disciplined self-fulfilment.

Children in the Home

But Jesus said, Suffer little children, and forbid them not, to come unto me: for of such is the kingdom of heaven.

—Matthew 19:14

One reason for urging young people to achieve a certain maturity before assuming the responsibilities of marriage, is the lack of ability on the part of the very young to assume and discharge the responsibilities of parenthood. The arrival of a baby often causes additional strain on the husband-wife relationship and, if the husband has been in the habit of running away from problems, sometimes results in desertion. Preparation for successful marriage should begin long before and continuing even after the wedding ceremony.

Any discussion of the problems of marriage and divorce must take note of the conflict betwen conjugal and illicit love. The marriage counselor is frequently confronted with problems growing out of relations between husband and wife, before and after marriage, and with the ties—of both love and blood—which unite parents and children. It should here be pointed out that for the most part in Christendom, and certainly in antiquity, the lot of the childless is looked upon as a grievous frustration. To be childless is not merely contrary to nature, but for pagan as well as Christian it constitutes a deep privation of a blessing which should grace the declining years of married life.

There are, of course, many couples who, for reasons beyond their control, are childless. We are sure the Lord will reward them in the life to come. But they who deliberately deprive themselves of the blessings of parenthood must abide the consequences and reap the rewards of selfishness.

On the ship of matrimony, where parents are the ship's officers, most of the passengers are children who were induced, without volition, to come aboard. Therefore, there is a binding obligation, fixed by law, both human and divine, to protect them even at the risk of life while they are in their parents' custody. To disregard this sacred charge, to desert or abandon them, is cowardly and culpable.

They who have experienced the joys—and occasional trials, tests, and sorrows—of bringing up a family, can imagine how pathetically incomplete the childless life must be. Each child brings its own contribution of affection, problems, and blessings, and each is a conduit from nature's inexhaustible reservoir of love.

Frequently parents of the first child are heard to ask, "How can I ever love another child as I do this one? All the love of which I am capable is lavished on this one, and if another or others should come, my love would have to be divided between or among them. Is it not better that this one have all my love and my undivided attention?" The answer to this question, of course, is that a person's capacity to love is increased in proportion to the number of persons to whom his feelings go out in parental affection.

As children come into the home, one notes a marked change in both husband and wife. The seriousness and permanence of their marital responsibilities are emphasized with

sobering effect. A new phase of education of the parents begins and, with this education, should come maturing adulthood.

Each child is a new link in the chain which binds husband and wife together. As father and mother lavish their affections on the child and become more fully aware that they have entered upon a joint enterprise in which they must share increasing responsibility, and co-operate in effort, they become more securely bound to each other, and the voluntary bonds that bind them together are with each new child more securely riveted. That this is true is shown by statistics. Happily married couples have more children than do the unhappy, and divorces are less frequent where there are several children in the home.

Children, with their spontaneous love and laughter, while they bring added duties and responsibilities, take away much of the humdrum of routine daily living, lend diversity to life, and, by awakening memories, make the parents young again.

Children tend to take our thoughts away from ourselves, help us to overcome self-centeredness and selfishness, and change the direction of our ambitions. In our children we proudly find some little reproduction of ourselves and see in them a sort of immortality. Therefore their welfare is of first importance. It is while the children are young that we establish the attitudes toward us which they will carry all through life and which will be reflected back to us in later years.

Too many people in this machine age seem to feel that children are a misfortune, an additional burden; in fact, someone has said, "Each child is for the mother a step

toward the grave; for the father, a step toward bankruptcy; and for both, a step toward misery." The fact is that the exact opposite of this is true. Women who have large families generally live longer than the unmarried or the childless. Biologically in many cases each child brings to the mother new vitality and to the father, because of the need for increased effort, greater earning power, and to both, if they assume their responsibilities with the proper attitude, there comes a happiness which the unmarried or the childless cannot know.

There is no more challenging, rewarding, or sacred mission in life than successful parenthood, bearing and rearing children, in partnership with God. Parents derive blessings, gain experience and education from their offspring which they can get in no other way.

We have been in homes where children were hushed and shushed into frightened silence, and where what little conversation there was between parents was either raucous disputation or montonous mumbling.

Some children's mental and spiritual growth is stunted by a pervading atmosphere of whimpering self-pity or the perpetual antagonisms of immature adults.

Some children are cowed into silence by unwise display of authority and the curtailment of any show of independent thinking. Any evidence of spirit or sprouting is arrested by rough and calloused handling, while the eager child is tapped on the head or forced to draw into a shell, as the final word of authority is spoken in anger.

In the home, of all places, there should be gracious and intelligent conversation in an atmosphere of comradeship, of good humor, and always of love.

In the good home we find a soil best suited for healthy growth, not only for children but for adults as well. Here, as in all gardens, the plants need constant nourishment and care and plenty of sunshine.

Unfortunately there are same immature minds in mature or large bodies. There are some parents who have not matured mentally, emotionally, and spiritually, and yet little children are, for the time being at least, wholly subject to them.

> The arresting and somewhat terrifying fact about the home is that in it new human beings are wholly at the disposal of the old. They come trailing clouds of glory; but what happens to these largely depends upon the adults who have the child in their control.
>
> —Overstreet

If, then, to marry and rear children is a sacred mission, which is to continue throughout eternity, they who marry and deliberately deprive themselves of children not only disregard a divine injunction but deprive themselves of priceless blessings and that joy which is the real object of our being. The Psalmist understood this when he said:

> Lo, children are an heritage of the Lord: . . .
> As arrows . . . in the hand of a mighty man; so are children of the youth.
> Happy is the man that hath his quiver full of them: . . .
>
> —Psalm 127:3-5

The Latter-day Saints believe in large families wherever it is possible to provide for the necessities of life, for the health and education of their children, and when the physical and mental health of the mother permits.

Sometimes only love can make endurable the otherwise bitter experiences of life. Therefore, as each child brings new love into the home, the parents are thereby fortified for what lies ahead. The parents with the largest families are, generally speaking, most successful in life's battle. They not only gain the love and confidence of their children, but through them retain some of the courage, not to say at times the audacity, of youth.

Each normal child is born with a question mark stamped upon his soul. He has from the first the habit of reaching out, inquiring, learning, seeking, and expecting to find answers to his questions. In the successful home this habit is encouraged, and it becomes fixed and continues in both thought and action. If his natural versatility is encouraged and strengthened, he will not be afraid in unfamiliar surroundings, he will tackle new problems with confidence. Sometimes we witness the tragedy of a "too busy" and irritable parent, dimming or rubbing out the question mark or turning it into a zero, making his existence tasteless, limited, and unproductive.

But nature refuses to be stifled, and the child is driven to seek answers elsewhere, to test his ingenuity in forbidden fields. It is here that some of the seeds of juvenile delinquency are sown—by unheeding parents.

I do not know of a better shrine before which a father or mother may kneel or stand than that of a sleeping child. I do not know of a holier place, a temple where one is more likely to come into closer touch with all that is infinitely good, where one may come nearer to seeing and feeling God. From that shrine come matins of love and laughter, of trust and cheer to bless the new day; and before

that shrine should fall our soft vespers, our grateful benedictions for the night. At the cot of a
sleeping babe all man-made ranks and inequalities
are ironed out, and all mandkind kneels reverently
before the living image of the Creator. To understand a child, to go back and grow up sympatheti-
cally with it, to hold its love and confidences, to
be accepted by it, without fear or restraint, as a
companion and playmate, is just about the greatest
good fortune that can come to any man or woman
in this world—and, perhaps, in any other world,
for all we know.

And I am passing this "confession" along to the
fathers who may be privileged to read it, and for
the benefit of all the "little fellers" — the growing,
earth-blessing little "Jimmies" and "Billys," and
"Marys" and "Janes" of this very good world of
ours.

—From article in *Valve World*

In-laws Get Off the Boat

In many cases the cause of divorce can be traced right to the doorstep of unwise in-laws. As each new marriage craft sets sail, there should be a warning call, which is familiar to all ocean travelers, "All ashore that's going ashore," whereupon all in-laws should get off the matrimonial boat and return only at infrequent intervals and then only as invited guests for brief visits. If they are wise and polite, they will remember they are merely guests and not members of the crew. They will make no comment on the condition or management of the ship and will leave the controls entirely in the hands of the captain and the mate. To do otherwise is to invite trouble for hosts and guests alike.

While it may be difficult for an experienced seaman to refrain from giving advice to young and inexperienced sailors, and while such advice might be welcome and helpful, there are occasions when permitting others to learn by experience is the wiser course. In-laws should resist the temptation to give gratuitous advice or to take the reins of discipline, which so often causes friction.

It is shocking to note that in these western states including Utah, almost one-third of all marriages end in divorce. Many of these could have been avoided if the in-laws had adopted a policy of "hands off."

In-law relationships can become a definite hazard. In-laws on both sides should try to determine whether they themselves are assets or liabilities in this new partnership,

and should always remember they serve best when they themselves are silent partners. They should especially be on guard against feelings of jealousy when they note the allegiance of their son or daughter to their respective mates. Parents should discourage rather than approve the tendency of some young people to employ the "tantrum technique" and "run to mother" for sympathy and advice. Should either mate run home after a spat he should be given some good advice and sent back where he belongs. Parents, because of their natural bias, should not undertake to arbitrate, nor take sides. Be on guard against creating or fostering actions or situations which result in divided or conflicting emotions or loyalties.

This rather blunt warning to in-laws is not intended to suggest or imply that once a son or daughter is married the parents are to take no further interest in them. Their interest and concern not only continues but increases, as each new in-law becomes a member of the family with claims to the first allegiance of your son or daughter.

Young persons often sit at my desk and detail the aggravating incidents of "meddling in-laws." But they are often embarrassed when asked, "And what kind of in-law are you?" The marriage ceremony has made "in-laws" of both bride and groom.

As newlyweds are welcomed into the wonderful world of married life, the in-laws on both sides should realize that some surrender, separation, and change of status is necessarily involved. It may be difficult for both old and young to make the adjustment, but it is nature's law.

In one of the Indian tribes in Canada, custom—doubtless born of experience—requires that mother-in-law and

son-in-law shall never speak or cross each other's paths after the wedding. If either breaks this rule, he must forfeit a pony to the other. There are few forfeits and few divorces in that tribe. We do not recommend such extreme measures but obviously the "in-law" problem is not new or unique.

The young couple should try to understand their new relatives, must expect them to be different from their own folks, and it is often a difference that is needed in the blood stream. This new relationship should never be approached with a "chip on the shoulder" attitude. After all, we do, in a sense, "marry the whole family." Your mate has the blood of your in-laws in his veins. He or she has inherited some of their characteristics, good and bad.

Most in-laws are assets rather than liabilities, depending on how they adjust to, accept, and are accepted by their new relatives. Young couples should accept their in-laws as they are. Neither one should make unfavorable comparisons between their respective families.

The proud young father should not be too touchy when the bride's mother tries to be helpful with the new-born babe. It is just possible she knows more about baby technique than he does. She has had some of her own, else he would not have his present wife. Let him add kindness to diplomacy and appreciate her help.

The in-law problem—the butt of so many silly jokes—would not be acute if all concerned would act intelligently and meet the problem on an adult level as sane grown-ups should: subdue their jealousies, control their tongues and tempers, and be grateful for the opportunity to become a part of a larger family.

At my desk one day, Alice sobbed, "His mother didn't like me from the beginning. She thinks no girl is good enough for her boy. I think she is jealous of me. She's breaking up our home."

Well, Alice, perhaps she is a bit jealous, as you will likely be twenty-five years from now when some young girl takes little Tim from you. You, too, may feel sure at that time that no girl in the world is good enough for Tim, but some sweet thing is going to get him. In fact, some other mother is now training that girl for him, and when they marry, the mother of that girl will be sure that Tim is not good enough for her little girl. Let the experience you are now having help to make a better mother-in-law of you.

Timothy, Sr., came in after Alice left and when asked what he thought was the main cause of their trouble, he said at once, "Her mother—she never weaned her daughter and insists on babying her and bossing me."

When the two were together at my desk, they were asked to make some self-appraisal. Each was asked, "What kind of in-law are you? Are you touchy (which is only conceit with a hair trigger), self-opinionated, quite sure you have all the answers? Are you faultless?"

Timothy and Alice were really very much in love, but were "kicking against the pricks" instead of making necessary adjustments. Since that time an interview with the respective in-laws resulted in a general understanding and at least a truce.

The most intimate relationships between husband and wife are too sacred to be discussed with others generally, even with one's parents, for they are the deepest expression of their love for each other. Counsel and advice may be sought from

parents, doctors, church leaders, marriage counselors, and others, but a discussion of the private lives of husband and wife is seldom in order. It is a bond between them and them alone. In those relationships each should remember the fundamental difference between male and female and neither expect the other to react in a way or follow a pattern not common to his sex. This is an area where giving of oneself, restraining oneself, considering the other before oneself, are fundamental to lasting happiness and complete spiritual union.

One fruitful cause of unhappy in-law relationships is the frequent need for two families to occupy the same house.

The Census Bureau reports that three million families in the United States share their home with a second family; in other words, six million families are doubled up. In such cases the causes of friction are vastly multiplied. Moving in with "the folks" or with others should be avoided wherever possible, but if there is no alternative, then precautionary measures and sane and sober planning are prerequisites to peace.

Whenever possible, young couples should arrange to live by themselves, even though it be in an inadequate house in a low rent area. The average young wife will be happier in one room though it be only partly or poorly furnished where she can be queen of that room than she would be with her husband's folks or even with her own. Moving in with "the folks" causes the bride to feel she is not really married, not independent, not grown-up, not wanted. She longs for privacy and primacy in her own home.

Where it becomes necessary to double up temporarily, then both the parents and the young couple should prepare

themselves for inevitable adjustments which joint occupancy involves.

There is no use pretending that two families can live in the same house without occasional difficulties, even one-family homes cannot always avoid them. There will be some inconvenience and occasional annoyance to all concerned, but this is true in all human relationships, but if there is a businesslike arrangement made beforehand and lived up to, much friction can be avoided.

There should be careful planning and agreements on such things as the use of the family car, sharing the use and expense of utilities, including radio and TV, entertaining friends, regular hours for meals, retiring, etc. A little forethought about little things which so often trigger explosions will reduce the danger.

Where there is no choice but for two families to live together, it is wise, where possible, to divide the house into two apartments, if only with a curtain, and even if the young couple must cook on an electric plate and put up with some inconvenience. Arrangements should be made for privacy, not alone in the bedroom but in the kitchen as well. Give the young wife the privilege of making decisions, making mistakes, burning the biscuits, crying over hurt feelings, and, in general, the privilege of growing up. No young married woman is content to be in another woman's house and be treated as a child or servant, even though the other woman be her own mother.

It would doubtless be easier for them to use the electric appliances of the parents, enjoy the spaciousness of the larger rooms, etc., but character is not developed or self-esteem maintained by dependence, by submitting to decisions

made by others without consultation, nor is the delicate technique of building a home acquired while eating meals prepared by others at a family table provided by others, or enjoying comforts without cost or obligation. The young husband wants an opportunity to appraise his wife's ability as a cook and homemaker, and the wife is anxious to demonstrate and improve her ability.

The in-law relationship can, by forethought and planning, coupled with self-control, become more smoothly cooperative and conjunctive, but it takes thought and effort on the part of all. It is a relationship that should be anticipated and prepared for with happy expectancy rather than approached with misgiving.

The bristling approach to any problem invites resistance and trouble. Sometimes when in-laws meet, the young and the old, their nerves seem to penetrate through their clothing and are supersensitive and super-charged. They may be goaded by petty vexations until they strike out at real or imaginary enemies with a venom all out of proportion to the provocation. In such cases, proximity should be cushioned with kindness and direct contact avoided until "the heat is off."

Let the in-laws, both young and old, relax, be normal, see in the enlarged family some new and wonderful people, and appreciate the improvement of the stock by transfusion of new blood. Let them refer to their new relatives as father, mother, son, or daughter from the wedding day on, and seek comradeship and confidence. Do not be like the young husband and father who, when asked how he referred to his mother-in-law, said, "During the first year I just said 'she' and after that I called her 'grandma.'"

There are, of course, some mothers-in-law who are tactless, loquacious, and meddling and some fathers-in-law who are taciturn, surly, and domineering; of these we hear very frequently though they are perhaps only one in a thousand. The other nine hundred and ninety-nine we take for granted.

But remember there are also some bad sons-in-law and daughters-in-law who must be endured by long-suffering parents. A little honest self-appraisal, followed by painstaking reform, might be beneficial to all.

The ideal parent-in-law will be an objective and neutral spectator when there are differences of opinion between the young husband and wife, will wait until asked before offering suggestions or giving advice, will treat juniors as equals (though it may entail a little imagination) and not as children to be reformed, will just let them *be* and become, will remember his own struggles and mistakes and be patient.

The ideal junior in-laws will remember that each was loved by parents before their own young love was born. They must not desire or attempt to displace that love but add to it by their own. They will, even at some personal sacrifice or inconvenience, make the senior in-laws feel at home and wanted; will praise and compliment them for the fine job they did in bringing up their own family, especially the one they have chosen for a life's companion. (Take tongue out of cheek and uncross fingers if the above is an expression of a wish instead of a fact.) Let all in-laws and members of families remember that tact, tolerance, consideration, and kindness are hallmarks of culture and that being civil is evidence that one is civilized.

When families, and the extension of families through marriage, can learn to get along harmoniously together, we shall have peace, and rather than calling for in-laws to get off the boat, they will be joyfully welcomed into the fleet where all may hear the blessed words, "Peace be still."

Finance

But godliness with contentment is great gain.

For we brought nothing into this world, and it is certain we can carry nothing out.

And having food and raiment let us be therewith content.

But they that will be rich fall into temptation and a snare, and into many foolish and hurtful lusts, which drown men in destruction and perdition. For the love of money is the root of all evil: . . .

—I Timothy 6:6-10

Family financing can be one of the most interesting, satisfying, and mutually educational factors in the many joint efforts of husband and wife. It continues to call for study and adjustment throughout married life if there is to be a successful and happy partnership, and this regardless of the economic bracket in which they operate.

The family that counsels together and agrees upon its budget and then lives within it will not only avoid unpleasant scenes when bills come due, but will know the joy and security of achieving a balanced budget at the end of the year, an ever-present challenge in family, state, and nation.

Budgeting, both income and outgo, discussing together and agreeing beforehand where economies are to be practiced, are essential to success and happiness in family life. Econo-

mies or savings should be wisely and fairly spread over necessary family expenditures—including the husband's—and not as is often the case, all pinched out of the wife's household expense account.

Husband and wife should consider together whether they can afford a new car, membership in expensive clubs, frequent dining out, or trips abroad. A frugal family will put aside a little every month and refuse to touch it except for emergencies. Children who learn lessons of thrift and industry at home will avoid a lot of trouble when they themselves undertake to manage the financial affairs of married life.

The husband who is avaricious, niggardly, stingy, secretive, and who refuses to disclose to his wife the amount of the family income, and to discuss with her how it can best be spent, overlooks the fact that marriage is a joint venture in which both partners are equally interested and in which both are investing their very lives.

The husband who refuses to take the wife into his confidence on money matters, on income, expenditures, and investments, and who makes her beg for every cent of money she spends, should not be surprised if his wife eventually asserts her independence, claims her rights as a human being and as a partner, and refuses longer to be treated as a little child. A man should be frugal but not penurious. Wives are entitled to dignity and consideration and not merely to penny-pinching indulgence.

Marriage should be a complete and a genuine love-inspired partnership, where each ascribes to the other not only maturity but also intelligence. For a man to deny

his wife her right to examine the joint balance sheet occasionally, is to imply that it is not jointly earned, or that she is not
intelligent enough to understand it. Generally such implications are false. No husband would stand for it if their
respective roles were reversed.

Every husband should know how impossible it is for
a wife to budget and spend wisely from the joint income if
she is not allowed to know how much she has to spend.
The wife who is taken into the confidence of the husband
on money matters will usually resist the temptation to be
extravagant or to gamble on the future by buying needless
things because they are cheap or can be obtained with little
or no down payment. The income of the average family,
meager though it may be, can be made to cover necessary
expenses. Also the wise husband will provide his wife with
a monthly allowance for personal needs, and this item in
the budget should not be audited.

The following is almost a verbatim account of part
of an interview in the writer's office with a husband and
wife who were contemplating divorce:

Question: (To the wife) What do you think is
the main cause of the unhappiness in your
home?

Answer: I think it has to do mostly with finances.
My husband, during twelve years of marriage,
has never given me one dollar for my personal
use. I have no allowance; I must go to him "cap
in hand" if I need a new dress or hat, and am
questioned and criticized as though I were a
teen-ager. I must account to him for every purchase made for the children and am frequently
scolded and humiliated before them. I'd rather

go without needed clothing than endure abuse.

I have never known what his income is and do not know anything about our holdings or our assets, but I know he buys a new car every year which I am not permitted to drive. I am allowed a limited and inadequate amount of credit at the grocery store, and get scolded and accused of extravagance when bills come in. I have no help in the house and work at least fourteen hours a day seven days a week without any holidays.

We have five children. The oldest is eleven, and none of them ever gets a nickle without an unpleasant episode. I am blamed for making them extravagant when, in fact, I submit every purchase to him before I buy.

I think it best that I get a divorce and have a definite monthly sum by court order before the children begin to leave home.

To Husband: What have you to say?

Answer: Well, I give them all their food and clothing and shelter and provide for their education.

Question: Do you include your wife as one of "them" to whom you "give" so much?

Answer: Certainly.

Question: Suppose you should lose her tomorrow? What would it cost you to hire a cook and housekeeper?

Answer: I have not considered it.

Question: How many hours do you work on the job?

Answer: Forty hours a week.

Question: Do you realize she works more than ninety hours a week and never sees a dollar to to call her own?

Answer: I hadn't realized.

Question: Do you consider her your wife or your servant?

Answer: I think she's my companion.

Question: Do you know that she is now preparing a declaration of independence, and that if open hostilities (divorce) result, the court will certainly rule in her favor?

Answer: I realize that.

Question: Would you be willing for even one month, to have your positions reversed; to double the hours in your work week and have no money to spend?

Answer: I didn't realize how unfair I've been.

Conclusion: There was no divorce.

Another serious oversight on the part of many husbands is the need for making provision for the partnership business to be carried on in case the "manager" should suddenly be taken out of the picture. Husbands who refuse to confide in their wives on financial matters should witness the pitiful and often tragic scenes in lawyers' or marriage counselors' offices when a grieving widow tells how all through their married life her late husband neglected or refused to let her know any of the details of his business—their business. She is not only forlorn and helpless, but also tragically unprepared for the sudden responsibility of "general manager," and she becomes an easy mark for scoundrels.

Lack of experience in meeting the problems of income and expenditure is recognized as one of the factors most frequently recurring when church officials or marriage coun-

selors search for the causes of broken homes. Daily decisions must be made on "to buy or not to buy" and what to buy.

When, because of lack of education, the earning power of the husband is below average and it is thought necessary for the wife to work, and, therefore, to postpone having a family, the couple should pause and seriously count the cost. Limiting families leads to many evils, physical, moral, and spiritual. How foolish is the couple who postpones or deprives themselves of life's choicest blessings in the name of economy, while at the same time indulging selfish, expensive habits or buying luxuries which lose their glamour and their value before they're paid for.

The young couple should remind themselves frequently that "if we buy this we can't have that." Let "this" represent an automobile and "that" a baby. Who would compare their value? The one depreciates and becomes worthless, but who can appraise the worth of a soul and especially if it is "of his own soul, a part?"

In connection with the economies of the home, the question of the mother working outside the home must be considered. That family makes a poor bargain which exchanges the real luxury of a mother's supervision and presence in the home for increased income and extravagant and non-essential expenditures which keeping up with the neighbors or the spirit of the times seem to demand. Paraphrasing a biblical text, "What does it profit a family, though they gain and furnish a house, be it ever so grand, and lose a home, be it ever so humble?"

Too often the young bride, or the older matron, cannot distinguish between essentials and luxuries, and insists upon the latter at the expense of the former. Both husband and

wife should be familiar with and practical about the fixed overhead expenses of the average family, i.e., rent, mortgage payments, food, utilities, clothing, hospitalization, insurance, etc. Each should be willing to deny himself some immediate wants in order that both may have security and be prepared for emergencies.

There are two ways of balancing any budget, whether it be national, state, or family. Balancing the family budget requires constant attention, skill, and dexterity. Any budget may be balanced by increasing the income and/or reducing expenditures. Too many recklessly allow expenditures to get out of control in optimistic anticipation of increased income.

A heavy and unnecessary drain on the family budget, which bores into the financial undergirdings of a home like termites in a house, is indulgence in the things which God and experience warn are not only unnecessary but are not good for man. Selfishly insisting on gratifying appetites or indulging habits, adds to the financial burden of the family, without adding anything to the health, happiness, or development of its members.

Unfortunately, practically all families are subjected to the ceaseless and seductive advertising of extravagant and harmful things. All the media of modern communication are employed to induce people, including children, to use things which are deleterious to health and happiness; they are made to appear desirable; and the children are often de- ceived into believing they are harmless and even essential to achieving adulthood. Surely the Lord saw our times when he warned against "The evils and designs which do and will exist in the hearts of conspiring men in the last days," and

He warned and forewarned us against the things which are not intended for the use of man. Observance of God's law of health would ease the heavy strain from many family budgets and make it possible to have other things which are health-promoting, joy-giving, and permanently satisfying.

Scientific investigation and medical research, as well as world-wide experience, have proved the cancerous and lethal effects of the products made and sold by conspiring corporations. They falsely claim to have filtered out the poison in cigarettes—thereby admitting its inherent and virulent presence. Promises of reduced amounts of poison, even if kept, would only prolong the process of undermining the health of the victim, while increasing the financial burden. Indulgence in liquor by either spouse threatens the security of the home and its inmates and often results in penury, loss of employment, broken homes, and juvenile delinquency.

Thrift and frugality are steppingstones to prosperity. Blessed are they who build them into the substructure of the home, for they shall have security. One of the strongest links in the matrimonial chain is a joint project of judicious economy, of systematic saving, where each makes sacrifice and practices self-control in the interest of future independence.

Be ambitious and enterprising but beware of avarice! Worshiping a golden calf—or a silver dollar—is as reprehensible today as it was when Moses condemned its appearance among the children of Israel.

> And he said unto them, Take heed, and beware of covetousness: for a man's life consisteth not in the abundance of the things which he possesseth.
> —Luke 12:15

Soft Discipline and Hard Knocks

Children, obey your parents in the Lord: for this
is right.
                                              —Ephesians 6:1

Some men are jealous of their prerogatives as the head
of the house, insisting that as such they have the exclusive
right to discipline the children — and sometimes the wife.

The scriptures in all ages join husband and wife together without distinction in requiring the obedience of the
children. The Decalogue enjoined:: "Honour thy father
and thy mother."
                                              —Exodus 20:12

We sometimes read of "Paternal authority." In most
cases it should be "Parental authority" for it is more justly
exercised and respected when both parents share its responsibility. In other words, both parents are charged with
the joint responsibility of discipline in the home.

While the children are young and lack judgment and
understanding, they should not be allowed to follow their
own wills or make their own decisions. Because of the
greater understanding and experience of the parents, the
children must be taught and required in kindness but with
firmness to respect and obey the will of the parents.

There is a continuing obligation for children to honor
their parents, for parents are instruments in God's great
design for continuing the race, and they have an obligation
to nourish, preserve and train their offspring. So the children have a perpetual obligation to honor their parents.

Dr. Adler says:

While there may be disagreements regarding the relation between husband and wife, there is none regarding   the inequality between parents and children during the offspring's immaturity. Be-cause children are truly inferior in competence, there would seem to be no injustice in their being ruled by their parents, or in the rule being absolute in the sense that children are precluded from ex-ercising a decisive voice in the conduct of their own or their family's affairs.

—The Great Ideas Syntopicon

Children must be taught from the beginning that there are certain rules governing the relationship of parent and child, upon the observance of which will depend not only the welfare of the new member of the family, but also the success of the joint undertaking to establish a home. Here, as in all of God's vast creations, obedience to law is funda-mental and pre-requisite to achieving the joy, attaining the goals, and receiving the rewards of immortality and eternal life.

It has been said that with the acquisition of power comes the temptation to misuse it.

We have learned by sad experience that it is the nature and disposition of almost all men, as soon as they get a little authority, as they suppose, they will immediately begin to exercise unrighteous dominion.   —D. & C. 121:39

We have spoken about soft discipline and must now say a word of warning against unrighteous dominion some-times leading to tyranny and excused in the name of disci-pline.

There is no room for bossism in married life, or for petty tyranny, where one or the other of the parents exer‐ cises unrighteous control or dominion over children, and/or the other spouse.

To be raised in or to live in an atmosphere of tyranny discourages ambition, saps mental and spiritual vitality, and transforms members of the family into subdued, crushed, and colorless beings. Sometimes harsh discpline leads to hypocrisy, deceit, lying, and trickery in an attempt to escape the tyranny which they do not have the courage or the opportunity to challenge openly.

The marriage counselor sometimes meets a husband of the timid type who is married to a domineering woman, and whose conversation consists chiefly of "me too," or "yes, my dear." The dominating spouse of either sex has a deadening and crushing effect upon his mate. Some men are unable to make up their minds on any question without childlike going to their wives for permission, or, in effect, getting his wife's countersignature on his pass. The wife who dominates her husband to that degree should not be surprised if he becomes deceitful and attempts to solve, by circuitous methods what he dare not face head on.

By the same token, the husband and father sometimes becomes domineering in his assertion of authority and plays the petty role of domestic dictator.

Both parties to a marriage should understand it to be a partnership, and not a proprietorship. Slavery has no place in the home. People will not long endure the dictates of a tyrant. The despot may demand obedience for a time, but his misused authority will be either openly challenged or defeated by covert rebellion. Even during the enforced

semblance of submission it is the nature of the human being to risk his life to protect his freedom. The oppressed and downtrodden are constantly planning escape, ever trying to outwit the tyrant. It is a sad commentary on family government and discipline when the children resort to subterfuge, evasion, and deception behind the backs of parents.

Sometimes fond mothers help children to cover up misdeeds for fear of the cruel punishment which a father's uncontrolled temper may prescribe. The best citizens do not come from homes where tyranny prevails or where its progeny—deception, evasiveness, lying, and rebellion—are spawned.

Enforcement of proper discipline need not, should not, and must not lead to the exercise of unrighteous dominion. They who have authority must always be on guard against the temptation to misuse it. Love grows best in the atmosphere of freedom, confidence, and trust.

A great leader once said, when asked how he governed his people, "I teach them correct principles and let them govern themselves." There are some homes which are over-governed.

It's a shame when children are raised to be cowards, have to tolerate injustice without protest, who have to endure years of suffering because they fear the consequences of asserting their rights. Husband or wife does himself and his spouse an injustice when he meekly yields to a domineering personality.

It should also be noted that bullies are generally cowards, and when challenged they will back down. Both partners in marriage should understand each other from the

beginning and should agree that neither will be required to "come to heel." It is much easier to meet this tendency in the beginning rather than to try to correct it after years of cowardly patience.

Let there be fine co-operation and loving companion- ship in the home, where each does his best for the good of all concerned, where love will be the only tyranny, and mutual service and respect are as the oil that will keep the lamp of love alight.

On the other hand, over-solicitude, babying, pampering, and attempting to shield children from all fear, frustration, and disapproval, often result in serious teen-age and later marital problems. The parent-child relationship should be studied constantly and faced with good old-fashioned "horse sense," else a child's growth may be warped, his emotional life distorted, and he himself finally become either an un- manageable roughneck or a sickly misfit. The child, boy or girl, who is babied and pampered through his childhood and adolescent years, will expect the same treatment from his mate when he marries; if he doesn't get it, he'll go whimper- ing back to his parents; and unless they have the kind of love that is compounded of fortitude, courage, and good sense, they may break up the marriage. Someone recently said: "A modern home is a place where everything is con- trolled by switches — except the children."

There came to a regiment in the world war a "spoiled brat" who had to learn obedience the hard way. He was an only son and had been babied and pampered from infancy until his chief characteristics were wilfulness, selfishness, and disobedience. He became problem number one in school; his days of truancy exceeded his attendance. The teacher did

not enforce obedience because she had been told by his parents that he was a nervous lad who needed gentle handling. After his second visit to the principal's office for insubordination he was expelled. In Sunday School he caused the resignation of several teachers and was finally asked by the bishop to stay away. Failing to qualify for high school, he joined the army.

During the first week in the army he tried to repeat some of his home, school, and Sunday School antics, and upon receiving his first direct order from the sergeant, a tough veteran of former wars, his reply was, "You go to ....!" This, of course, made the old sergeant see red. He placed him under arrest and took him to the commanding officer under guard in spite of vociferous protests. He was told he had the right to elect between a court martial and a summary trial. He told the commanding officer to do whatever he .... pleased as he was going to quit the army anyway.

The patient officer advised him that one does not quit the army as he might quit school. He was in the army for at least three years, and there was a war on. He was insolent and defiant and was sentenced to thirty days of severe discipline. At the end of the first week of punishment the prisoner asked the sergeant to take him to the C.O. again. The sergeant informed him that prisoners' appointments with the commanding officer must be requested twenty-four hours in advance, so he had another day of "training." When he finally came before the officer, he stood at attention, saluted smartly, and said, "Sir, I'll obey every order given me while I am in this army." Feeling that the man had learned his lesson, the officer remitted the balance of the sentence and

placed him on probation. The soft discipline of his parents resulted in some very hard knocks.

Two years later this man was corporal of the guard in France, near the front lines, and the officer, now a colonel in another regiment, and member of the general's staff, was on a tour of inspection. The young corporal asked permission to speak to him and this is what he said, after saluting, "I want you to know, sir, that the lesson in obedience which I learned from you when I joined the army saved my life recently. If I had not learned to obey orders implicitly, I would have left my post while under fire and would have been shot as a deserter."

In a recent editorial in the *Deseret News*, the following was quoted:

> "From a Texas Police department leaflet — Twelve Rules for Raising *Delinquent* Children. How well do they apply?
>
> "1.   Begin with infancy to give the child everything he wants. In this way he will grow up to believe the world owes him a living.
>
> "2.   When he picks up bad words, laugh at him. This will make him think he's cute. It will also encourage him to pick up 'cuter' phrases that will blow off the top of your head later.
>
> "3.   Never give him any spiritual training. Wait 'till he is 21 and then let him 'decide for himself.'
>
> "4.   Avoid use of the word 'wrong.' It may develop a guilt complex. This will condition him to believe, later, when he is arrested for stealing a car, that society is against him and he is being persecuted.

"5. Pick up everything he leaves lying around — books, shoes and clothing. Do everything for him so he will be experienced in throwing all responsibility onto others.

"6. Let him read any printed matter he can get his hands on. Be careful that the silverware and drinking glasses are sterilized but let his mind feast on garbage.

"7. Quarrel frequently in the presence of your children. In this way they will not be too shocked when the home is broken up later.

"8. Give a child all the spending money he wants. Never let him earn his own. Why should he have things as tough as YOU had them?

"9. Satisfy his every craving for food, drink, and comfort. See that every sensual desire is gratified. Denial may lead to harmful frustration.

"10. Take his part against neighbors, teachers, and policemen. They are all prejudiced against your child.

"11. When he gets into real trouble, apologize for yourself by saying, 'I never could do anything with him.'

"12. Prepare for a life of grief. You will be apt to have it."

Young parents often feel that their parents and grandparents were Victorian in their outlook, and they themselves are determined to get rid of the old-fashoned approach to parent-child relationships, but they fail to realize that there are certain old-fashioned values which are time-tested. Older parents may be behind the times, but it should be remembered that during the time that is behind them, some valuable and enduring lessons were learned.

There should be no surrender of the limited but God-given sovereignty of parenthood. Young parents should prayerfully seek wisdom in the exercise of discipline. Erratic and apologetic discipline, interspersed with pussyfooting, often leads to defiance, lawlessness, to the juvenile court or to jail. Parents must have the courage and the genius to incline the twig with kindness but with firmness — and to use if need be.

Parents must be more than mere attending psychiatrists. Your children came into your home, it is hoped, because you wanted them, and they are entitled not only to your love but also to your tender but firm guidance and discipline. The habits of conduct which they form in their early years will carry over into their married lives. Every child should know there are some things he must not and cannot do, and that for every broken law there is a penalty. He should also know that there are some things he cannot have, even though he cries for them. How frequently do parents, saddened by experience, vainly wish they had been wise before the event, and taught lessons in self-denial, self-control, obedience, and honesty. The Lord himself finds it necessary to deny us some things for which we ask and occasionally even allows us to be hurt for our own good. In later life we thank Him for the wisdom of His love.

President McKay gives the following counsel:

Let us never lose sight of the principle of obedience. Obedience is heaven's first law, and it is the law of the home. There can be no true happiness in the home without obedience — obedience obtained, not through physical force, but through the divine element of love. Love draws from husband and wife and from children to parents that

blessed obedience and compliance that make life worth while.

* * *

Learn the value of self-control. You are never sorry for the word unspoken. I believe the lack of self-control is one of the most common contributing factors of unhappiness and discord. We see something in the other which we dislike. It is easy to condemn it. And that condemnatory word arouses ill feeling. If we see it, and we refrain from speaking, in a few moments all is concord and peace instead of animosity and ill will. Controlling the tongue is one of the greatest contributing factors to concord in the home, and one which too many of us fail to develop.

I think the children should be properly directed and controlled, not permitted to run around without any limitation to their actions as they affect other members of the household. Do I mean that you should be cruel to that child? No! That you should whip a child? No! It is unnecessary. But it means that when you say "no," you mean what you say.

—*Pathways to Happiness,* pp. 118, 120

Parenthood is one of life's most serious and challenging responsibilities but also the most permanently rewarding if carefully prepared for and courageously and prayerfully discharged. Parents should exercise authority in righteousness, "reproving at times with sharpness and then showing an increase of love."

J. Edgar Hoover, who has spent a lifetime dealing with undisciplined misfits and criminals, gives good advice on parental authority in *American Mercury,* February 1958:

"Shall I make my child go to Sunday School and Church? Yes! And with no further discussion about the matter. Startled? Why? How do you answer Junior when he comes to breakfast on Monday morning and announces to you that he is not going to school any more? You know! Junior goes.

"How do you answer when Junior comes in very much besmudged and says, 'I'm not going to take a bath.' Junior bathes, doesn't he?

"Why all this timidity, then, in the realm of his spiritual guidance and growth? Going to let him wait and decide what Church he'll go to when he's old enough? Quit your kidding! You didn't wait until you were old enough. You don't wait until he is old enough to decide whether he wants to go to school or not to start his education. You don't wait until he is old enough to decide whether he wants to be clean or dirty, do you? You don't wait until he is old enough to decide if he wants to take his medicine when he is sick, do you?

"What shall we say when Junior announces he doesn't like to go to Sunday School and Church? That's an easy one to answer. Just be consistent. Tell him, 'Junior, in our house we all go to Church and to Sunday School, and that includes you.'

Your firmness and example will furnish a bridge over which youthful rebellion may travel into rich and satisfying experience in personal religious living. The parents of America can strike a telling blow against the forces that contribute to our juvenile delinquency, if our mothers and fathers will take their children to Sunday School and Church regularly."

Married men and women may be relatively successful in one or several fields of activity and find satisfaction therein, but however successful they may be, if they fail in the central and ultimate role of parenthood, all other successes whatsoever will not satisfy the human heart, nor qualify men for celestial glory. The sacred obligation of parenthood involves not only becoming partners with each other and with God in the creation of new life in mortality, but it imposes the responsibility of being His agents in training and directing the activities of youth. Parents must become companions, guides, counselors, disciplinarians, and judges, and for their stewardship they must account to our Heavenly Father. The poor excuse sometimes heard, "Because of my love for him I just could not discipline him," will not satisfy the Divine Judge, whose discipline is undeviating and whose laws are inexorable and immutable.

Struggle and Strength

The brightest crowns that are worn in heaven
have been tried and smelted and polished and
glorified through the furnace of tribulation.

—Carlyle

The reason we include a chapter in this book on marriage under the title, Struggle and Strength, is that happy
and successful marriages are not usually found in coddled
luxury and ease. Furthermore, the lifetime undertaking of
building a home and rearing a family calls for courage, fortitude, and faith, and sometimes the very experiences which
people call adversity are the ones that make us strong and
capable. The storms of adversity, like those on the ocean,
bring faculties into use, require invention, prudence, and
skill. Many of the talents revealed in the great would have
lain dormant but for adversity. Just as hammer and chisel
are needed to bring the statue out of the block, so adversity,
if courageously met, will bring out the man.

When troubles come in the home, and come they will,
whether they be economic, loss of health, bereavement, or
tragedy, husband and wife and family must clasp hands, close
ranks, and with faith in God carry on. Someone has said,
"we must learn to spread our wings to the lifting winds of
adversity." Homer and Milton, two of the greatest of
the poets, were blind. The Apostle Paul said he spent his
life with a thorn in his side, and it was said of Jesus, "Though

He were a son, yet learned he obedience by the things which
he suffered."

> "Heaven is not gained by a single bound;
> But we build the ladder by which we rise
> From the lowly earth to the vaulted skies,
> And mounts to its summit round by round."
>
> —Joseph Gilbert Holland

If you sometimes wish for comfort and ease, wealth
and affluence, and think you can get them without struggle,
just go out and put some oil on the railroad track and note
what removing the friction does to locomotion. All of us
have witnessed instances where emergencies made giants out
of little men.

A disastrous fire which destroys the house, loss of a
fortune or of a benefactor, or other events which knock the
props from under men, are often the very things that cause
them to buckle down and develop the latent powers within
them.

The following paragraph is taken from the book *Rising
in the World or Architects of Fate* by Orison Swett Marden,
published by T. Y. Crowell and Co., New York:

> . . . "Robinson Crusoe" was written in prison.
> The "Pilgrim's Progress" appeared in Bedford Jail.
> The "Life and Times" of Baxter, Eliot's "Mon-
> archia of Man," and Penn's "No Cross, No
> Crown," were written by prisoners. Sir Walter
> Raleigh wrote "The History of the World" during
> his imprisonment of thirteen years. Luther trans-
> lated the Bible while confined in the Castle of
> Wartburg. For twenty years Dante worked in
> exile, and even under sentence of death. His works
> were burned in public after his death: but genius
> will not burn.

The purpose of citing instances where men have risen through struggle is to encourage young parents to teach their children by precept and example how to work, to struggle with and overcome difficulties, to teach them self-confidence, —and let them get their own homework.

Most older men are grateful for the difficulties which beset their pathway. Often they would have gone in one direction, but God willed it otherwise. They were hoping for the comfort and ease which they thought would come with wealth. Being denied and forced to struggle they developed those qualities which would later be needed. The pruning of a fruit tree gets rid of surplus wood, increases the yield, and improves the quality of the fruit.

Raising a family under any condition is a difficult task. It calls for constancy, patience, inventiveness, and skill, and through it all husband and wife must stand together. As long as they press forward hand in hand and heart to heart, nothing can happen to them which, with God's help, they cannot handle. But if they lose confidence in each other, separate and try to face life's trials alone, they not only will meet disappointment individually, but will ruin the very project to which they were willing at the beginning to give their lives.

We recommend to all young married couples that as soon as possible after marriage they make a start on their own, they refuse to lean on their parents, except for counsel and advice, and, avoiding rashness, be unafraid to venture. With faith in themselves and in each other, they can and will succeed, and each success will qualify them to meet the next encounter. It has been said that there are ten thousand chances to one that genius, talent, and virtue shall issue from

a farmhouse rather than from a palace. Uinterrupted success and prosperity seldom qualify men for usefulness or for happiness. As someone has observed, "Too much sunshine made the desert." We never go into the Scandinavian countries without remembering that the north wind made the Vikings. As Browning said, "Then welcome each rebuff that turns earth's smoothness rough, each sting that bids not sit or stand, but go."

We are suggesting that you do not bow down to adversity, but that you treat it as the golfer treats the bunker. He tries by skill to avoid it, but if he cannot, he fights his way out. The unquenchable spirit is the mark of a man.

And let the young couple, both man and woman, be unafraid of hard work. Most good qualities which we admire in others were developed by industry.

The English statesman, William A. Gladstone, at the end of his life, said, "I have found my greatest happiness in labor. I early formed the habit of industry and it has been its own reward."

We summarize the following story by Orison Swett Marden:

> A rich man's son of fifteen told his father he was tired of studying and thought it unnecessary as his father had plenty of money.

> The father told him he need not go to school if he was not willing to study but he must go to work as he must not be idle.

> The next morning his father took him to visit a prison where he asked for an interview with a former schoolmate. After exchanging greetings the prisoner said, "I suppose this is your son."

"Yes," said the father, "he is just about the age we were when we went to school together. What happened to bring you here? When I saw you last your prospects were much better than mine."

"It's a short story," said the prisoner, "My ruin was caused by idleness and bad company. I would not study. I thought there was no need for a rich man's son to do that. Father died and left me great wealth, of which I never earned a dollar. The money soon went and I awoke to find myself poorer than the lowest clerk in the house. I did not know how to get a dollar by honest labor so I tried to get it without work. The rest needs no telling."

The prisoner went back to his cell and the father asked the warden how many of the prisoners had ever been trained to any useful work and was told, "Not one in ten."

On the way home the son was thoughtful and his father said, "You seemed surprised when I said you must work. This visit to the prison is my answer—I am a rich man but not rich enough to have you live without work. Many a father has learned to his sorrow what it is to have an idle son."

The boy answered, "I think I'll go back to school."

There is an ancient saying that the gods sell all pleasures at the price of toil. Longfellow declared that the secret studies of the poet are the sunken piers on which his poetic work rests; out of sight, but essential. Bryant wrote *Thanatopsis* one hundred times and was still dissatisfied with it.

"It is wonderful how many great successes have come by accident," said a friend to Rufus Choate. "Nonsense,"

replied the great lawyer, "You might as well let drop the Greek alphabet, and expect to pick up the 'Iliad'."

Alexander Hamilton said: "All the genius I know anything about is hard work."

Drudgery has been called "the gray angel of success."

> After I have completed an invention, I seem to lose interest in it. One might think that the money value of an invention constitutes its reward to the man who loves his work. But, speaking for myself, I can honestly say this is not so. Life was never more full of joy to me, than when, a poor boy, I began to think out improvements in telegraphy, and to experiment with the cheapest and crudest appliances. But now that I have all the appliances I need, and am my own master, I continue to find my greatest pleasure, and so my reward, in the work that precedes what the world calls success.
>
> —Thomas A. Edison

We are frequently called upon to counsel families whose homes are breaking up because of internal dissension, bickerings and strife. In many such cases, the family is in the higher economic brackets, and has all the essentials and most of the luxuries of life. But they are denied the blessings hidden in hard work and struggle, which are so essential to the development of strength. Hard work is often the best antidote for bickering and contention in the home.

Adversity and need for hard work often have an effect on the family similar to what happens in a nation at war. Experience shows that when there is a common enemy or a common danger, the people of a nation unite. Petty differences, and political parties are forgotten, and the pressure

from without has the effect of fusing the citizens into closer companionship, where the welfare of the whole becomes the concern of each individual. Often under such circum-stances real brotherhood becomes a fact in the nation.

What is true in a nation may also be true in a family. If the family meets crises standing shoulder to shoulder, they may prove to be a benediction in uniting and welding them into a unit. Disappointment, loss, sorrow, and bereavement help people to forget their petty differences and to recognize the imperative need for co-operation, loyalty, and unity in life's greatest undertaking.

In later years, the family who has passed through crises together will look back and be grateful for them; they were blessings in disguise. When the family are struggling toward a common goal, overcoming difficulties, recovering from sorrow and bereavement, they are able to transmute sorrow, contention, and strife into joy, peace, and harmony.

Successful men, in all lines of activity, proudly tell the story of their early struggles and attribute their success to the strength that came therefrom.

One purpose in life is to learn how to face troubles and difficulties and opposition, but in married life these experi-ences must be faced together, must be met with a united front, for here as in warfare, the enemy attempts to divide and conquer.

In almost every home there are days when dark clouds hang low, when, in sickness or bereavement, the hand of affliction plucks at the heart strings. It is then that father and mother must meet life's problems with hands clasped and hearts united, and when children note such unity, the whole family takes new courage and hope, and they become an unbeatable unit.

Let each young couple then, know from the beginning
of their married life, that some stormy days lie ahead, that
some differences of opinion will arise, that some difficulties
must be met and overcome, that they themselves must be
purified by fire, and let them be unafraid of life.

Be strong!
We are not here to play, to dream, to drift,
We have hard work to do, and loads to lift.
Shun not the struggle, face it, 'tis God's gift.

Be strong!
Say not the days are evil—who's to blame!
And fold the hands and acquiesce—O shame!
Stand up, speak out, and bravely, in God's name.

Be strong!
It matters not how deep entrenched the wrong.
How hard the battle goes, the day, how long;
Faint not, fight on! To-morrow comes the song.

—Maltbie D. Babcock

The Waste of Worry

It is not work that kills men; it is worry. Work is healthy; you can hardly put more upon a man than he can bear. Worry is rust upon the blade. It is not revolution that destroys the machine, but the friction. Fear secretes acids; but love and trust are sweet juices.

—Henry Ward Beecher

As Dr. Herbert Popenoe points out in his handbook *Now You're in College,* "Worry involves no reason, no judgment, no plannings for future contingencies. It is just plain worry and it is as pernicious as it is widespread — and unnecessary."

"There are only two reasons for worry:

"Either you are successful or you are not successful. If you are successful there is nothing to worry about; if you are not successful there are only two things to worry about. Your health is either good or you're sick; if your health is good there is nothing to worry about; if you are sick there are only two things to worry about. You are either going to get well or you are going to die; if you are going to get well there is nothing to worry about; if you are going to die there are two things to worry about. You are either going to heaven or you are not going to heaven; and if you are going to heaven there is nothing to worry about; if you are going to the other place you will be so busy shaking hands with old friends you won't have time to worry—so why worry?"

When Mandy, who had a tale of woe, was told, "There's no use in worrying," she replied:

"How come dere's no use in worryin'? When de good Lawd send me tribulation He 'spect me to tribulate, ain't He?"

The trouble with many people who are given to worrying is that they are fatalists. They say they just can't help it because they are born that way. The fact is, it comes to be a mental habit and if not corrected will, as many habits do, become a temperamental tyrant, spreading gloom, apprehension, and unhappiness. One who insists on sharing his morbid apprehension of future troubles with everyone he meets is a boring companion, an ungracious host, and an unwelcome guest.

> God always gives us strength to bear our troubles day by day; but He never calculated on our piling the troubles past and those to come, on top of those of today.
>
> —Elbert Hubbard

After all, people, as a rule, do not worry about present problems. They go to work and solve them. They have undue solicitude and anxiety about possible eventualities of the future. They imagine what may or may not happen, and in anticipation live through non-existent difficulties, keeping themselves poor by insisting upon mortgaging the future and paying interest in advance despite the fact that it may never accrue. Habitual worrying makes a person miserable in the midst of happiness. As one old lady said, "I always feel bad when I feel good because I know I am going to feel afterwards." Worry is 90% fear, which is the opposite of faith.

There is no fear in love; but perfect love casteth
out fear: because fear hath torment. He that fear-
eth is not made perfect in love.

—I John 4:18

The worrier is self-centered, preoccupied, and gloomy.
His short-circuited mind burns out the fuse, and the lights
go out. He seems to enjoy being miserable and insists on
others sharing his despair. He refuses to be comforted as
that would rob him of his cherished pastime. Worry is a
daytime nightmare and often has no more substance than a
dream. Every person can live one day at a time, but he who
insists on anticipating the future increases today's burdens
and disqualifies himself for tomorrow's duties. He does not
solve or reduce the future's problems, but rather saps his
mental, spiritual, and physical strength until when tomorrow
does arrive—and when it does it will be today, a better
day than he anticipated — he is much less able to cope with
it. Having dissipated his strength, lowered his vitality
through loss of sleep, lost his courage, he approaches "today"
in fear and trembling. And then in a vain attempt to justify
yesterday's worry he makes today miserable by borrowing
trouble from another tomorrow. Will Rogers once said:
"Don't let yesterday use up too much of today."

Reinhold Niebuhr penned the following prayer:

Give me the serenity to accept what can't be
changed; give me the courage to change what can
be changed; and the wisdom to know one from the
other.

Every couple should make wise provisions for the future, should plan that future together, make such provision
as is possible for emergencies, and then approach it with

unfaltering faith. It is possible to open a savings account of courage, faith, and fortitude to draw on as the need may arise.

Every person should forget the mistakes of yester-day, start each day with the accumulated knowledge of the past and with the confidence that comes from recognizing and correcting his mistakes, regain self confidence and carry on.

> There is a peace which cometh after sorrow,
> A peace of hope surrendered, not fulfilled.
> A peace that looketh not upon the morrow,
> But backward, on the storm already stilled.
> It is the peace in sacrifice secluded,
> The peace that is from inward conflict free,
> 'Tis not the peace which over Eden brooded,
> But that which triumphed in Gethsemane.

Some people do what a wise father, who was a farmer, warned his son against as he assigned to him the task of un-loading a ton of wheat and carrying it into a bin several steps up from the wagon. The wheat was contained in one-hundred-pound sacks. The father asked the son if he could carry that ton of wheat up those steps and put it in the bin. The son replied, "I think I can." The father then said, "But it weighs a ton; how will you do it?" and the son re-plied, "One sack at a time." "When you take one sack, which is about all you can carry, and, having climbed the steps are ready to dump it into the bin, will you worry about the nineteen sacks that still remain in the wagon, and be-cause of that worry forget to dump the one you have on your shoulder, carry it back down the steps and get another and try to carry both at the same time?" The son replied, "Of course not, I'd dump each sack and forget it. I know

I can carry all of them—one at a time." The father then wisely said, "Let that be a lesson to you through life. If you carry unhappy memories of yesterday, add them to the problems of today, and overload yourself with worry about tomorrow, you are as foolish as the man, who, trying to un-load the wheat, would carry the first full sack back to the wagon, take on the burden of another, and so continue until completely exhausted and the job unfinished."

> If pleasures are greatest in anticipation, just re-member that this is also true of trouble.
>
> —Elbert Hubbard

Worry and discontent, fretting and stewing, cease-less anxiety, unhappy dispositions, all tend to obscure the sun of happiness and like the fog and smog in some cities, shut out the sunlight and change daytime into night.

Let us throw open the windows of the soul, let in the sunshine of faith, take a deep breath, and tell all about us it is good to be alive. Truly "A merry heart doeth good like a medicine." Remember the saying, "Every time a sheep bleats it loses a mouthful, and every time we complain we lose a blessing."

Worry is more exhausting than work. It upsets the whole system, it fills the mouth with wormwood, the mind with apprehension, and the soul with despair. The best anti-dote for worry is hard work, which is invigorating and health-giving. To quote from Orison Swett Marden, in *The Secret of Achievement*, published by T. Y. Crowell and Co., New York:

> We can make life very largely what we wish, through education and control of the will. The bright, cheerful man makes a cheerful world around

him. The melancholy, morose, fretful, disjointed, sarcastic, critical, dyspeptic, bilious, gloomy man creates a world about him which is the reflection of his own mood. Some people have the power of making summer wherever they go. They infuse light and joy and happiness and beauty into everybody they meet. If you meet one of them on the street, he will throw a stream of sunlight into your soul which will light up the whole day. Others carry discord, gloom, despair everywhere. If they talk with you but a minute, they will manage to cast a dark shadow across the whole day, and send a chill through your body. One has the power of making the best of everything, of not only looking at the bright, but the brightest, side of things. He finds peace and comfort everywhere. The servants are all attentive. He is never snubbed. Everybody is considerate. Another is always being insulted, cut, slighted, neglected. We get pretty nearly what we give in this world, and we are treated about as we treat others. If others are uncharitable, neglectful, and unkind in their treatment of us, it is usually but the reflection of our own bad tempers and lack of charity.

Worry is wasteful, so *why worry?*

Divorce, a Social Evil

The Pharisees also came unto him, tempting him, and saying unto him, Is it lawful for a man to put away his wife for every cause?

And he answered and said unto them, Have ye not read, that he which made them at the beginning made them male and female,

And said, For this cause shall a man leave father and mother, and shall cleave to his wife: and they twain shall be one flesh?

Wherefore they are no more twain, but one flesh. What therefore God hath joined us together, let not man put asunder.

—Matthew 19:3-6

Divorce, which is an insidious social evil, is becoming epidemic in the United States, and is increasing dangerously in the Church itself.

Husbands and wives, fathers and mothers, should be constantly on guard against the symptoms of this growing evil. Misunderstandings that go unresolved, hurt feelings that go unsalved, harsh words that go unrecalled or unrepented of, often because of pride and stubborness, are forerunners of divorce. When these are not corrected, where there is continuing friction, increasing tension, and general unhappiness in the home, it is time for mental, emotional, and spiritual housecleaning, and each spouse should examine himself. Actually the couple who live in such an atmosphere are not really married, but only undivorced.

There are more than one thousand divorces every day of the year in the United States of America. This number would be doubled if we add to it the large numbers of desertions and those who are living apart without legal action— not divorced but un-married. This indicates a need for someone to call attention again to the menacing social evil of divorce or marriage failure.

The alarming and ever-increasing divorce rate in the United States is one of the most serious problems confronting parents, churches, schools, and society at large. In some western states, including Utah and Idaho, one third of all marriages end in divorce.

Too many people seek relief in the divorce courts without stopping to ask, "And now what?" "What do you propose to do when you are 'free'?" Remember, you will not be free from your own weaknesses of character, bad habits, neuroses, quick tempers, etc., which helped to wreck your home. If you are young, you will probably marry again, and you will take into that new venture these seeds of failure, as will your companions; and remember, neither of you will marry an angel.

Emotional immaturity, childishness, failure to behave as grown-ups are high on the list of causes of divorce. Let each person ask himself, "To what extent do these things apply to me?" and then let each one be honest with himself. Shallow ills bring tears of sorrow, but there are deeper griefs which plunge their plowshares into the hearts of men. One of them is divorce. It is often met dry-eyed, but it sears not the eyes alone but the heart as well.

When considering divorce, parents must not forget that God has entrusted little children to their keeping—at

their request—and He will hold them responsible for their stewardship. Parents will be answerable in the final outcome, not only for the direct consequences of their broken homes, but indirectly for future divorces as well, for the example set for children in the home of their childhood may be followed by them in later years. We cannot endanger or wreck the future lives of children with impunity.

In the case of desertion, marriage counselors find it difficult to determine causes and prescribe remedies. In cases of divorce, the court records are available, but in desertion, where the husband simply disappears, marriage counselors and welfare agencies generally know nothing about it until the wife appears at some community agency seeking for support.

> But if any provide not for his own, and specially
> for those of his own house, he hath denied the
> faith, and is worse than the infidel.
>
> I Timothy 5:8

In a recent conversation with some of the district court judges, they referred to the heart-breaking, unhappy results of divorce—poverty, lawlessness, and juvenile delinquency are often traceable to broken homes. Their recommendation is that minimum age laws should be heeded by parents. These same judges refer to the immaturity of young couples. The lack of religious conviction and activity, the financial failure and insecurity in their parents' homes are contributing causes of premature marriages, which so often end in divorce.

The hasty resort to the surgery of the divorce court is tragically foolish. Simple remedies and preventive measures are generally available. Too often a spouse fails or refuses to

obtain the help of trained and interested specialists who might save his marriage.

How foolish would be the mariner who, when sailing in dangerous waters, waited until his ship went on the rocks before calling for a pilot. After the ship has hit the rocks the pilot, who might have prevented the accident, sometimes finds himself almost helpless in the face of irreparable damage.

So in marriage, it is of the utmost importance that the young couple, figuratively the captain and the mate, consult the pilot (parents, church leaders, professional advisers) before they set sail; get a chart, often a spiritual chart, of the vast oceans which lie ahead. Rashness where life and death are at stake is inexcusable and tragic. We cannot over-emphasize the need for pre-marital counseling.

Husbands and wives, fathers and mothers, Church officials and marriage counselors, as well as law-making bodies, should be alerted to the dangers of this spreading malady. Divorce generally creates more problems than it solves. Many resort to it as an exit without inquiring, "What's on the other side of the exit door?" One cause for marriage failure is the fact that civil divorces are easy to get, and another is that jobs for women are generally available. These two facts often cause the wife to assert her independence, overcome erstwhile caution, lose her fear of consequences and cast scruples and obligations aside.

Unfortunately, divorce does not have the universal stigma that it once had. Young people do not fear its consequences. In fact, some of the young people seem to enter the front door of marriage only if they can look through and see the back door of divorce wide open. In other words, they are not willing to play for keeps.

Choosing the divorce court as a way out unless there are justifiable grounds often indicates a tendency to run away from obligations and to refuse to face facts. There is a solemn duty on the part of parents to find a way to make their marriage work, to isolate and examine the causes of discord and apply appropriate remedies in the pure air of frank discussion, willing compromise, and mutual penitence. Unjustified divorce is like voluntary bankruptcy. It adver-tises failure, leaves unsatisfied creditors, and makes a new start difficult because of lowered self-confidence and reduced credit rating.

Some fathers, shirking responsibility, and being un-willing to make the sacrifices entailed by family life, coward-ly desert the ship and figuratively take to the lifeboats during a storm and leave their wives and children to drift un-attended. On the real ocean, only cowards desert a ship dur-ing a storm or a battle; desertion is almost next to treason. To seek what seems to be an easy way out of marriage with-out ample justification is to brand oneself as a quitter, as selfish and unreliable, especially if there are children in the home.

A divorcee, having failed once, will lack faith in the out-come as he tries marriage again, and will not have the con-fidence of his friends, or possibly of his new spouse, who, knowing of his first failure, will have misgivings. Also, the divorcee is not as young as he was formerly. He has given some of the best years of his life to his mate and his family, and what he has left is all he can offer to another. Few people are content to have secondhand goods. When the divorcee, man or woman, gleefully announces, "I'm in the market again," his friends are liable to think, if they do not say, "Yes, in the used car market."

The by-products of divorce are loneliness, frustration, the pity of friends, and a feeling of no longer belonging. How often the divorcee, man or woman, who is responsible for it wishes, with heartbroken regret, he had tried a little harder to make a success of an admittedly difficult task, and thereby avoided the catastrophe of divorce.

Just as the marriage ceremony is only the beginning of a long journey, requiring faith, fortitude, courage, determina- tion, so divorce is often only the first step to a series of heart- breaking misfortunes, not only for the principals but espe- cially for the children, who are innocent victims. If you reply that you will bring to your second venture the lessons learned in your early experiences, we suggest it would be better to try these new methods on the spouse you already have. It may be even more difficult to get along with the new spouse.

> When souls that should agree to will the same,
> To have one common object for their wishes,
> Look different ways, regardless of each other,
> Think what a train of wretchedness ensues!
>
> —Rowe

In a technical sense there is no such thing as a "temple divorce." Divorce is a civil decree granted by the courts of the land. But, after a civil divorce has been granted to a couple who were married in the temple, application may be made to the President of the Church for a cancellation of the sealings involved. But this power to loose is exercised only when circumstances are serious enough to justify it. The Church does not countenance divorce, except where conditions or conduct warrant it.

The President of the Church has said:

In the light of scripture, ancient and modern, we are justified in concluding that Christ's ideal pertaining to marriage is the unbroken home, and conditions that cause divorce are violations of His divine teachings. Some of these are:

Unfaithfulness on the part of either the husband or wife, or both, habitual drunkenness, physical violence, long imprisonment that disgraces the wife and family, the union of an innocent girl to a reprobate — in these and perhaps other cases there may be circumstances which make the continuance of the marriage state a greater evil than divorce. But these are extreme cases—they are the mistakes, the calamities in the realm of marriage. If we could remove them I would say there never should be a divorce. It is Christ's ideal that home and marriage should be perpetual—eternal.

The number of broken marriages can be reduced if couples realize even before they approach the altar that marriage is a state of mutual service, a state of giving as well as of receiving, and that each must give of himself or herself to the utmost.

V. The Ripening Years

The Family, an Eternal Unit

"IT IS NOT GOOD FOR MAN TO BE ALONE"
HERE OR HEREAFTER

If, in the wisdom of God, it is not good for man to be alone in this world, is it not likely that He has made provision for continued companionship in the next world and throughout eternity?

Marriage was the first God-ordained institution among men. If it is to endure it must be founded on love, and as love is eternal, therefore, that which is begotten and sustained by love, the family, should be eternal.

There is no activity or relationship in life which brings men and women as near to Godhood as does successful parenthood.

When a man and woman undertake to build a home— not merely a house—and rear a family, they lay the foundation of what may become an eternal and ever-increasing kingdom, over which they may preside as king and queen forever. Obviously, if a couple agree in the marriage ceremony that the home and family are to remain intact, that is, to endure, only so long as the two of them shall live, then the relationship, and that growing out of it, is temporary and transitory; upon the death of either party to the agreement that family unit is dissolved, not only by the terms of the agreement itself, but by official pronouncement. Such marriages are binding and perfectly legal and honorable during

this life, but they are "Of no efficacy, virtue or force in and after the resurrection from the dead."

> Therefore, if a man marry him a wife in the world, and he marry her not by me nor by my word, and he covenant with her so long as he is in the world and she with him, their covenant and marriage are not of force when they are dead, and when they are out of the world; therefore, they are not bound by any law when they are out of the world.
>
> —D. & C: 132:15

God is love, and love is of God. It is greater than faith or hope, and it is intended to endure forever. It beareth, believeth, hopeth and endureth all things. It never faileth. (See I Corinthians 13)

But, as love finds its truest expression in the family relationship, obviously that relationship must continue after death else love will not continue to find full expression. Surely the love of God for His children—and here too we have a family relationship, for He is our Father — will continue forever. If, then, the family is to become an eternal unit, it must be built on an eternal foundation. It must be solemnized, ratified, and sealed by proper authority, and the parties thereto who keep their covenants and endure to the end shall have immortality, eternal life and eternal increase.

The Lord Himself said, "All covenants, contracts, obligations, vows and associations, etc., to be effectve in the hereafter, must be entered into and sealed by the Holy Spirit of Promise, by one who is appointed to hold this power." A contract which is to extend into the domain of the hereafter, and be binding throughout eternity, must be

validated by an authority superior to any which can be conferred by earthly governments.

Young people and all members of the Church should note and remember that the Lord said there is, "*Never but one on the earth at a time* on whom this power and the keys of this priesthood are conferred." This, of course, refers to the President of the Church, and while he may delegate others to act for him temporarily, he alone remains responsible. No man can take this honor unto himself. It should also be noted that no man to whom the President of the Church may give this special authority can transmit or delegate it to another. There is a legal maxim which says, "*delegatus non potest delegare*," which means a delegate cannot delegate, that is, transfer, his powers.

Because marriage makes possible the most intimate association of the sexes, under divine sanction, because "the hearthstone is the keystone of our civilization," because good people come from good homes, and because people need divine assistance to discharge the responsibilities and endure the irritations and strains common to married life, and finally, because marriage was originally intended to be eternal and everlasting, it should be validated by divine authority.

Celestial marriage enables worthy parents to perform a transcendentally beautiful and vital service as priest and priestess in the temple of the home. This training will help to prepare them for the exalted position of king and queen in the world to come, where they may reign over their posterity in an ever-expanding kingdom.

Children born of parents who were married in a temple for time and eternity are known as children of the covenant. There is no need for further rite of adoption or sealing. They

are spoken of as having been "born under the covenant" and this relationship of parent and child is of eternal duration. Therefore, to the Latter-day Saints, the family is an eternal unit.

If the married couple will keep in mind the long-range program which celestial marriage envisions and never lose sight of the glorious goal toward which they work, they will be able to overlook or overcome temporary obstacles as well as each other's idosyncrasies and make of life a glorious adventure.

They who are properly mated, who have the same faith, hope, and ambition and who keep alive their love for each other throughout life, will welcome the demands of parenthood, the long hours and the sacrifices entailed, and will consider every duty a privilege, and every obligation an opportunity.

That marriage is a precarious undertaking is evidenced by the fact that only two-thirds of the marriages are successful—and the word *successful* is relative. But life also is precarious and yet all the sons of God shouted for joy at its prospect. Marriage and the home lie at the very basis of purposeful living. It is pre-requisite to the realization of complete happiness in this life and the attainment of the highest glory in the world to come.

If our young people fully understood this lofty concept of marriage, they would consider no other. They would not be interested in elaborate ceremony, pageantry, or social prestige, but would enter into it in a spirit of reverence, devotion, and dedication. They would seek to become worthy to enter His holy house, make most sacred covenants and be married for time and eternity.

The Lord has made provision for all His children who will qualify to become partners with Him in His continuing creative work. He declared that His work and His glory is to bring to pass the immortality and eternal life of man. There await all who are faithful to the covenants made at the altar of celestial marriage a crown of glory, immortality, eternal life, and eternal increase, including increase of knowl-edge, intelligence, power, and dominion, transcendentally greater than anything man has known or can contemplate. But as previously stated, all blessings are predicated upon obedience to law. The Lord said:

And speaking of those who comply with the law and "are sealed by the Holy Spirit of promise" the revelation con-tinues:

> For all who will have a blessing at my hands shall abide the law which was appointed for that blessing, and the conditions thereof, as were insti-tuted from before the foundation of the world.
>
> —D. & C. 132:5

> They are they who are priests and kings, who have received of his fulness, and of his glory;
>
> And are priests of the Most High, after the order of Melchizedek, which was after the order of Enoch, which was after the order of the Only Begotten Son.
>
> Wherefore, all things are theirs, whether life or death, or things present, or things to come, all are theirs and they are Christ's, and Christ is God's.
>
> And they shall overcome all things.

* * *

These shall dwell in the presence of God and his Christ forever and ever.

These are they whom he shall bring with him, when he shall come in the clouds of heaven to reign on the earth over his people.

These are they who shall have part in the first resurrection.

*   *   *

These are they whose names are written in heaven, where God and Christ are the judge of all.

These are they who are just men made perfect through Jesus the mediator of the new covenant, who wrought out this perfect atonement through the shedding of his own blood.

These are they whose bodies are celestial, whose glory is that of the sun, even the glory of God, the highest of all, whose glory the sun of the firmament is written of as being typical.

—*Ibid.,* 76:54-70

The Apostle Paul said:

The Spirit itself beareth witness with our spirit, that we are the children of God:

And if children, then heirs; heirs of God, and joint-heirs with Christ; if so be that we suffer with him, that we may be also glorified together.

—Romans 8:16-17

And John, in his first Epistle, wrote:

Beloved, now are we the sons of God, and it doth not yet appear what we shall be: but we know that, when he shall appear, we shall be like him: for we shall see him as he is.

—I John 3:2

Surely all who understand this celestial law, with its guarantees if eternal life, eternal association with loved ones in the presence of God and Christ, forever and ever," will be satisfied with nothing less. Surely the blandishments of worldly possessions and associations which hold no promise beyond the grave—and which are so often disappointing even in this life—will have no appeal to any Latter-day Saint.

May God bless the youth of the Church with wisdom to take the longer view, to reject the temporary and transitory, however alluring, and have the vision, faith and courage to keep morally clean, to be worthy to marry in the temple and thereafter to earn the incomparable blessings of eternal associations with loved ones *for time and all eternity.*

Coming Into the Harbor

It is too late! Ah, nothing is too late
Till the tired heart shall cease to palpitate.
Cato learned Greek at eighty; Sophocles
Wrote his grand Oedipus, and Simonides
Bore off the prize of verse from his compeers,
When each had numbered more than fourscore
      years, . . .
Chaucer, at Woodstock with the nightingales,
At sixty wrote the Canterbury Tales;
Goethe at Weimar, toiling to the last,
Completed *Faust* when eighty years were past.
These are indeed exceptions, but they show
How far the gulf-stream of our youth may flow
Into the arctic regions of our lives . . .
For age is opportunity no less
Than youth itself, though in another dress,
And as the evening twilight fades away
The sky is filled with stars, invisible by day.

            —Henry Wadsworth Longfellow

When Longfellow wrote the above lines and read them at the fiftieth anniversary of his graduating class, he entitled the longer poem "Morituri Salutamus," meaning, "We who are about to die salute you." This was the gladiators' salutation to Caesar as they went into the arena to engage in mortal combat.

It is hoped that the choice of this poem, with its rather somber title, will not be taken to indicate that we older ones have lost our zest for living. We have traveled in strange

lands, been on many surging seas in all kinds of weather, and the lessons learned along the way help us to anticipate the later years with relish. Each new adventure has its excite-ment and its own rewards.

Older people may come into the quieter waters of maturity with hope and expectation unabated and with full assurance that the Pilot who has guided them thus far is still at the helm and that the greatest voyage is still ahead. Age is inexorable and invincible, but age can abound with satisfactions and delights if we retain unsatiated appetites for life's bounties and are sensitive to its continued blessings.

It is possible for men and women to condition them-selves along the way for the changes and adjustments which the passage of time requires. They who look upon middle and later life with joyful anticipation rather than with fear and dread will carry into each phase of life increasing wis-dom, experience, and appreciation.

It is possible for people to continue to participate crea-tively in the activities of life as long as life shall last, and this is relatively true, even among those who may be ill, crippled, or disabled. It is largely a matter of mental attitude, courage, fortitude, and faith. There is no arbitrary mile-stone, where active life must stop and old age and retirement begin.

Numerous examples can be cited of men 70, 80, or 90 years of age who undertake new projects which require years of active work to complete, and they live to finish the job, and do it with distinction. We could cite artists, philos-ophers, statesmen, church leaders, and others who have made rich contributions long after the time when laws or regula-tions would have turned them out to pasture.

Some of those who carry on creatively into these later years have been handicapped throughout their lives but it seems to matter little whether men have health or wealth or pedigree if there are ingenuity and courage. They who are strong of heart do not allow poverty nor riches to deter or deflect their ambition, or abate their tireless energy.

Older people are generally more kind and thoughtful, more emotionally sensitive and mature. They, like all of us, hunger for human contact and understanding, wish to feel needed, wanted, and useful. They have kept their curiosity alive, have an increasing awareness and have refused to limit their interests or lower their sights. Though they are older they are very much alive, still have a creative urge, are not dead to emotional reaction, and still hunger and thirst for knowledge and accomplishment. Many older people are justly proud of the fact that they got their second wind at 70 or 80 and, with the accumulated wisdom of the earlier years, are just learning how to live.

Looking back and thinking of the rewards along the way, and every period of life had its rewards, we see that adventure was the reward of youth, and that accomplishment and self-mastery made maturity worth while. We remember the planting and the sprouting times, the blossoms and the ripening of fruit. But though memory is freighted with nostalgia, we would not go back again even if we could, for the road ahead holds more promise, more excitement, more assurance, than any we have known. "Youth is the tassel and silken flowers of love; age is the full corn, ripe and solid in the ear."

Remembered best are the plowing and the planting time of life, but now we enjoy the ripened fields of grain. The creative miracles of life and nature are the things we can't

forget and, having seen them many times, we have the calm assurance that no winter will obliterate or long hold back the spring of immortality, for death is not the end of life, but rather its beginning.

We who are privileged, occasionally, to associate with some stalwarts in the Church who have exceeded by more than ten years the threescore and ten allotted unto man, are encouraged and inspired as we see them carry on with heads erect and souls undaunted. We note the inspiration of their leadership and are led to repeat again with Browning, "The last of life for which the first was made." Here we see authoritative influence wielded with patient deliberation and prudent counsel. They are, "tall men who live above the fog."

These men have rich qualities of soul and character which experience has brought to full fruition. As they quietly approach life's harbor, their silver heads seem to pierce the clouds and, living in two worlds, they interpret life to us.

These older ones who have retained their zest for living, and who still serve their fellow men with increased devotion and effectiveness, are crowned with serenity, tranquility, and peace. Though they are in the evening of life there is no evidence of the setting of the sun, but rather the bright aurora which heralds another and a better day. To them the wheels of life move onward; they know no retrograde movement.

In addition to their serenity, these men have gained perspective with a sense of values twice refined. They, with Emerson, have come to know "what the centuries say against the hours." Another jewel in their crown of old age is simplicity; fewer wants, and richer values. They are rich in

wisdom and full of counsel for the youth. In fact, their lengthened life is a continuing benediction.

From them we learn that advancing age is not a final landing port, that each station is for refueling and checking visas. And though we all make some mistakes, the time is too precious to indulge in vain regret.

These patriarchal prophets have no fear of death, for they know that He who has lighted their pathway through these many years has not suddenly ceased to be nor lost His interest in them.

There are and have been great women, too, who have lived beyond the fourscore ten allotted unto man. They attained ripeness without old age — a good woman never grows old — and were an inspiration to all who knew them. They were women of virtue because of the benevolence which dwelt in their hearts.

In the Church we think of the mother of the Prophet; of Eliza R. Snow, Zina D. H. Young, Emmeline B. Wells, Ruth May Fox, and others who have gone to their reward.

But the most loved and honored woman in the Church today is Emma Rae McKay, who at age eighty-two, is the ideal of all the women of the Church, and who, after their sixty-two years together, is still the sweetheart and inspiration of our beloved President.

With these and other examples of how life should be lived, and of the richness and the glory of the later harvest years, let the young married couples of our land take heart, clasp hands, and carry on together in faith and righteousness. They must endure to the end which alone assures immortality, eternal life, and eternal increase. Eternal increase

connotes not posterity alone, but the increase of power, of awareness, of wisdom, understanding, and intelligence, and, in fact, increase of all the qualities that make for Godhood.

This is no fallow field through which we travel,
   No barren land made waste by nature's rust;
This is no grassless plain where sand and gravel
   Are trod upon and ground to atom dust.

This is, instead, the fertile field of living,
   Where you and I have scattered precious seed;
Where we have raised affection, and are giving,
   One to the other, what our spirits need.

Our grain is cut—the loam of life is mellow,
   A kindly sun is beaming from above.
We've reaped abundant years of ripened yellow,
   For crops are rich when two have planted love.

—William W. Pratt

(Copyright 1945 by *Saturday Evening Post*)

D1505441